Paul Peacock has written books on making your own cheese and sausages as well as a wide range of other titles on cookery and vegetable gardening. An occasional panellist for BBC Radio 4's *Gardeners' Question Time*, he also writes a regular gardening column for the *Daily Mirror* as 'Mr Digwell' and has contributed to countless gardening and cookery magazines.

Also available from Constable & Robinson

30 Herbs for Your Kitchen Garden
Making Jellied Preserves
The Beekeeper's Field Guide
The Bee Garden
Organic Vegetable Growing
Grandma's Ways for Modern Days
Making Your Own Cheese
Chickens, Ducks and Bees
How To Make Your Own Sausages

MAKE YOUR OWN
BACON AND HAM
and other salted, smoked and cured meats

Paul Peacock

A How To Book

ROBINSON

First published in Great Britain in 2016 by Robinson

Copyright © Paul Peacock, 2016
1 3 5 7 9 8 6 4 2

The moral right of the author has been asserted.

All rights reserved.
No part of this publication may be reproduced, stored in a retrieval system, or transmitted, in any form, or by any means, without the prior permission in writing of the publisher, nor be otherwise circulated in any form of binding or cover other than that in which it is published and without a similar condition including this condition being imposed on the subsequent purchaser.

Important Note
When home curing, it is particularly important to keep all equipment, implements and surfaces completely clean and sterilised. In no circumstances can the publisher or author accept any legal responsibility or liability for any loss or damage (including personal injury) arising from any error or omission from the information contained in this book, or from the reader failing properly and accurately to follow any instructions contained in the book.

A CIP catalogue record for this book is available from the British Library.

ISBN 978-1-84528-592-0 (paperback)

Typeset by Mousemat Design
Printed and bound in Great Britain by CPI Group (UK) Ltd, Croydon CR0 4YY
Papers used by Robinson are from well-managed
forests and other responsible sources

Robinson
is an imprint of
Little, Brown Book Group
Carmelite House, 50 Victoria Embankment, London EC4Y 0DZ

An Hachette UK Company
www.hachette.co.uk

www.littlebrown.co.uk

How To Books are published by Robinson, an imprint of Little, Brown Book Group. We welcome proposals from authors who have first-hand experience of their subjects. Please set out the aims of your book, its target market and its suggested contents in an email to Nikki.Read@howtobooks.co.uk

This book is dedicated to Derek Senior,
whose friendly eagerness to try out new curing recipes
and his ability to produce amazing hams, bacons
and all manner of cured delicacies
is legendary.

Contents

Acknowledgements	xi
Preface	xii
1 Getting started	**1**
What is charcuterie and why bother doing it?	1
Enjoying unadulterated food	3
Some equipment you might find useful	4
Chemicals used in curing	13
The bare minimum	15
2 Introduction to bacon and ham	**16**
Bacon: How it is made and used	16
Pancetta: How it is made and used	17
Prosciutto: How it is made and used	18
Ham: How it is made and used	19
Recipes for cures	20
Using honey or syrup in curing	24
3 Bacon curing	**25**
Bacon: how it is made and used	25
Bacon recipes	26
4 Making pancetta	**50**
What is pancetta?	50
A little history	50
Pancetta: how it is made and used	51
Recipes for pancetta dishes	53
5 Making prosciutto	**61**
How to make a basic air-dried prosciutto	61
Parma ham	66
Making a Parma ham alternative	67

A note on hams from around the world	67
Recipes for proscuitto	73

6 Wet curing and cooking ham — 76

The best-flavoured meat for ham	76
Boiled or roast ham cure	77
How to cook a ham	80
Variations on boiled ham	81
Ham recipes	84

7 Curing beef — 88

How to make corned beef	89
How to make pastrami	93
How to make pressed beef	95
How to make biltong and jerky	96
How to make bresaola	99
How to make ox tongue	102
Recipes for cured beef products	105

8 Potted meats, pâtés and confits — 110

Using fat to preserve meat and offal	110
Pâté recipes	112
Confit	114
Rillettes	116
Potted meat	118
Galantine	123

9 Miscellaneous curing recipes — 126

Brawn	127
Collard pork	129
Chicken roll	130
Derek Senior's turkey and chicken ham	132
Derek Senior's slicing pork	133
Pressed meats	133
Bacon ribs	135
Pies for preserving	137
Raised pork pie	138

Sausage meat	142
Venison roll	144
Kofta	145
Pickled heart	146
Low and slow BBQ ribs	148
10 How curing works	**150**
The curing process	150
How salt preserves	151
How saltpetre preserves	153
Types of curing salt	154
Different cures for different processes	155
How much cure to use	156
Non-salt preservation of meat	157
11 Cuts of meat	**160**
Grain of meat	160
The types of muscle and quality of meat	161
Various cuts of meat	161
Pork joints and cuts	162
Beef joints and cuts	165
Poultry and game	168
12 Notes on smoking	**171**
Cold smoking	172
DIY smokehouses	173
Woods for smoking	174
How to cold smoke	176
Cold smoking for everyone	177
Light smoking	177
Powdered smoke	178
Hot smoking	179
Dutch oven	180
In conclusion	181
Recipe index	xxx
Index	xxx

Acknowledgements

The length of time it took to write this book, owing to illness, left it shelved, unshelved, started again, moped about, worried about and finally brought to a conclusion. Without the support of Giles Lewis and Nikki Read of How To Books and the patience of their colleagues at Little, Brown Book Group and Jane Donovan, freelance editor, this book would not have been completed, and for this I owe them my sincere thanks.

Quite literally, writing this book has been a beacon on my long road to recovery.

Preface

My first attempt at curing was a great success in one way, and a miserable failure in another. I had decided to make some bacon – having already tried cheese making, this seemed to be a reasonable next step on the steady march towards making our own food. It all worked out properly, the final product was tasty and for the first time ever we had bacon that could only be described as a million times better than the stuff bought in the supermarket.

So why was it a failure? Well, I worried about it all the time, and for days after we ate the bacon too. Could it be possible that this was something that would not spoil with such a small amount of salt? Had I made it too salty and my curing experiment would prove to be just an expensive waste of time with an inedible product at the end of the process?

I confess worry spoilt my first curing experience dreadfully. But that was twenty years ago and although I am still anxious about cures, no sleep is lost, and I am always completely thrilled with what I produce – even when I sometimes make mistakes.

Curing meat, a lifelong game of chess where you are always thinking and experimenting, has become one of the cornerstones of our family. Whenever one or other of the children returns home, the first thing they ask for in meal terms is a 'bacon butty', knowing of course that it's Dad's bacon and not supermarket's best plastic wrapped.

We grew an international Olympic weightlifter on food like biltong and ham, and visitors to our home have come to expect some homemade treats – I think my most successful experiment was a lighthouse pie, which consisted of a fried slice cut with a ring to be the same size as a slice of homemade black pudding. A similarly trimmed piece of thick-cut dry, cured bacon, again made at home, and a fried egg from one of our hens were cooked in the same ring cutter used to cut the bread, black pudding and bacon. The whole dish was piled up like a lighthouse with the yolk at the top. I was so proud you'd have thought I'd won the Nobel Prize!

Starting out in curing meat is an adventure that will literally change your life. It did mine, and the only regret I have is not starting to cure in earlier years. I thought it was something that was only possible in food factories. The truth is quite the opposite. Every ingredient we eat started life in someone's kitchen, and still the very best food is created in the same way. The proper place for drying ham, a batch of biltong or a side of bacon is a suitably cool, protected part of your home, where you and only you have control of what goes into the meat and what comes out too.

Making your own cured products gives you an opportunity. Yes, you can make the best food for the same price as the moderately priced packaged products in the supermarket, but you can also make it a whole lot healthier too! For example, you can control the saltiness of your bacon and you don't need to add chemicals to maintain the stability of the product on some shelf, you simply create something special, *healthily* special.

Until recently my wife Diana and I travelled the country teaching people how to make food ingredients from scratch and frequently taught at the Women's Institute Cookery School at Denman in Oxfordshire. Perhaps my proudest moment was when we made some overnight bacon – the recipe is featured in this book on pages 27–8, and cooked it for the college to try. One venerable lady in tweed said it was 'Bacon as it used to be.' You couldn't get prouder and for the first time in years my chest was puffed out more than what I call my waist.

And that's the whole point of this book. Food is about two things: love and pride. Curers have plenty of both.

Chapter 1

Getting Started

In this chapter we'll look at charcuterie and why we should bother doing it and then what kind of equipment and chemicals you'll need to get started.

What is charcuterie and why bother doing it?

Charcuterie is actually a French word that simply means the cutting of meat. More than just butchering, it comes from a society that generally could not afford to kill an animal to consume the whole beast in a few days, or at one sitting, such as a royal court with so many mouths to feed. It implies the cutting of meat so that it can be preserved, dried, extended, made more of, and, perhaps most important of all, enjoyed.

It's not just about preserving but flavour

The ancient art of curing and smoking food has made an enormous contribution to human development. What was once a necessity has become a treasure-trove of delicacies, amazing ingredients, meats that can arguably be much superior to the original, allowing people to plan and schedule hunting and farming and to create surpluses for later consumption. It is a good job that cured meats are so tasty. Maybe human society would have crashed and burned had they been horrid!

That is the whole point of this book. In the past I have written books that implored readers to take up gardening or sausage or cheese making because they are great tools for survival and one day they may need this half-forgotten knowledge. Not so this book; it's about flavour and fun.

Of course there are many, many recipes for the survivalist who wishes to set his larder with food to last all year, but here we are concentrating on flavour, and I have no apology to offer for including recipes based purely on their taste. With this in mind I have included recipes for the barbecue – not ordinarily thought of as curing, but often food that is salted and smoked, and yes, it does preserve too. There are pies, pâtés, confits, sandwich meats, hocks, brawn, hams and bacon, pastrami and corned beef, jerky and biltong, kebabs and faggots; also meats from the ancient world. Together, we will traverse the Silk Road and look into Turkey, Greece, Italy, Spain, Africa and Central Europe, India and China, South, Central and North America.

Modifying meat by curing or smoking it, adding flavours and making the dishes we love today is not possible without an array of techniques and materials, but surprisingly little in the way of equipment is needed, save a sharp knife, pans and bowls. Smoking is more complex, but, equally, needn't be too onerous on the wallet.

There are various methods of making stock, rendering fat and the correct use of herbs (both for flavour and their preserving effect) for the production of jellies for pies and pâtés; and the use of cuts of meat such as pigs' trotters, heads, cockerel comb and, of course, the wonderful offal so long ignored.

Learning from your mistakes

I hope this book will provide you with some inspiration. One final note: it is full of mistakes. These are quite deliberate and are solely the author's. Where in the past I have attempted to make a certain product and it has all gone wrong, I'll let you know, because you learn from mistakes – especially when someone else makes them.

Here is an example just to whet your appetite. I was making a ham so I made a simple cure of salt and sugar and rubbed it into the meat, then poured more cure over the ham in a lidded plastic box. At this point I noticed a small crack in the box and thought to myself, 'Well, no bacteria will bother the meat because it's covered in salt.' Actually, a few days later, the box was full of maggots! A fly had crawled into the box, laid its eggs, and they didn't seem to mind the salt at all! Perhaps they were just a little thirsty after their salty dinner.

Obviously, no one wants a maggoty ham and so it had to be discarded. It just goes to show how amazing it is that life always takes advantage of the resources it finds, and how important it is that we make sure we follow a robust Health & Safety regime, which should include the purchase of an electronic fly zapper if you intend to make a lot of homemade products or wish to sell your products.

Enjoying unadulterated food

It is a sign of the times that unadulterated food is something to be desired, almost as though it is something to which one should aspire. This never was the experience of even the poorest people of our grandparents' day. Of course there was less food, including a lot less meat, but what there was generally came fresh and unadulterated with shelf-life-extending chemicals, colourants and goodness knows what else. Today it is the norm for food to be pumped with hormones, dusted with pesticides, and in many parts of the world it is genetically altered too.

Certainly the number of additives added to food continues to grow. There are now enzymes and residual flavour-enhancing chemicals added to food that are not covered by labelling legislation. Enzymes are considered to be food preparation aids, and not on the list of ingredients on the packaging. The original enzymic food preparation is cheese, using rennet, an enzyme, to coagulate the protein in milk. However, modern enzymes are used to get as much meat as possible from the carcass, to add flavour, to maintain colour, texture and flavour and even to create flavour where there was none – in the production of fake meats.

It is not unusual to find sliced ham with a large proportion of chicken, where an enzyme is added to the product to make it taste like ham, making it cheaper. Indeed, you can buy chicken that tastes hammier than best York ham! If you buy sliced meats in the supermarket wrapped in plastic, it's a good idea to study the ingredients first. When making your own cured products, you can always be sure of the very best, and that is what we are striving for here. I can personally guarantee your own bacon will be better, oh so much better, than that sold by some of the most illustrious shops in the UK. A designer hamper is not nearly so good!

Some equipment you might find useful

Charcuterie is unlike other hobbies in that it not only produces something to eat, it becomes a way of life, an extension of a love affair with food. The bacon maker often wants to progress to making his own sausages, cheese and bread. It's a fascination that grows on you. It is like other hobbies in that the good ones have kit to buy and discuss –which tool is best for this and that process – and eventually people accumulate lots of equipment in the pursuit of perfection. But I don't want to give the wrong impression here – it is possible to cure meat and make the most extensive variety of meat products using very rudimentary equipment, such as a plastic bowl and a sharp knife.

Sterilising and cleansing

One of the first things you should be sure to have in place is a good sterilising system. This can be something simple – a large heatproof bowl for boiling water for metal objects, maybe a supply of sterilising tablets for non-metallic items and even a steaming system for cleansing knives and utensils. You can buy non-chemical-based sterilisers that are often used for babies bottles and associated equipment, and these are perfectly suitable.

You will need to sterilise worktops too. I do this by wiping with vinegar and then sprinkling salt over the dampened area. Afterwards I wipe it clean with a new, clean towel.

When working with meat, always wear a freshly laundered large apron. It's not going over the top to buy a butcher's overcoat, maybe even a butcher's hat, and neoprene gloves, which come in bulk packs. It is important that you keep everything as clean and sterile as possible. Butcher's coats, hats and a lot more equipment besides can be readily purchased from the numerous butcher's supplies companies on the internet.

Knives

The more you can invest in a good set of knives, the better. Expensive knives are not just a luxury, they are made from the best-quality steel, which is able to withstand sharpening time and again. Along with a set of knives, buy a steel (used for putting an edge on knives) and learn how to use it properly. A steel is basically a circular rasp used for sharpening knives. Whenever a knife is used, microscopic alterations in the edge of the knife appear, which blunt it. The steel is not there to give the knife an edge – it simply repairs the one it already has.

Always remember a steel does not make a blunt or damaged knife sharp. It simply gives a sharp knife that extra sharpness needed to do its work efficiently. Blunt or damaged knives should be repaired or discarded.

Using a steel

A steel is a metal pole with serrations all around, giving the appearance of a circular file. It has a handle and knife guard and is used to sharpen knives. Steels should be used daily to maintain knives. They should be grease-free too, so always make sure your knives are clean and dry before using the steel – any amount of grease will clog up the steel and make it inoperative. The basic rules are: draw the cutting edge of the knife forwards at an angle of about sixteen degrees and bring it along the whole length of the steel. Repeat for both sides of the knife. Don't try to sharpen too quickly – you will get a rhythm with practice. However, the technique you use should not really matter so long as the knife is sharpened by repeated and alternate (first one side, then the other) strokes. Some people put the steel end on a worktop and then draw the knife across it, others hold the steel in one hand and flash the knife over it with the other. Choose whatever method works best for you.

If you need to sharpen halfway through cutting, wash and dry the knife in hot soapy water before using the steel.

Most charcuterie courses include sections on knifecraft.

Boning knife

This is a short-bladed curved knife that is used for removing meat from close to bones, and for separating cuts of meat. Usually they are flexible, allowing you to cut a clean surface as close to a bone as possible. A clean cut means the meat will last longer, whereas rough cuts tend to promote bacterial growth by increasing surface area.

Avoid the temptation to be overzealous in trying to remove every last gram of meat from the bone – anything left will produce better stock once the bones are boiled.

Butcher's knife
If you can manage it, buy two sizes of knife: 18cm and 28cm, for the general cutting of meat. They are used for cutting through muscle and skin, the larger one being somewhat heavier, and with a sharp edge it will cut very cleanly indeed.

Chef's knife
This is a multi-purpose knife, usually with a curve on the blade, with a reasonably heavy stock to give weight to operations such as slicing through vegetables. It is generally a cutting knife rather than a chopping knife, and my preference is to use a specifically designed vegetable knife for preparing herbs and spices as well as general vegetable preparation.

Slicing knife
Used for cutting meat and sausage, the slicing knife is straight-bladed, about 25cm long and sometimes serrated. It is a broad knife, allowing you to set the vertical in the cut more easily. Often mistaken for a bread knife, this knife really is a must for ideal presentation of your hard work. It is particularly useful when you need to cut thin slices of bacon, prosciutto and ham.

Cleaver
Some people use nothing else, especially the flat-bladed Chinese style cleaver that lends itself to every conceivable use in the kitchen. In Western cuisine, cleavers are for breaking through small bones and a butcher's saw is used for cutting through larger ones. Quartering rabbit and chicken is an ideal job for a cleaver.

I would always recommend the use of a chain glove for your free hand when using a cleaver – and any knives for that matter. Being hit on the fingers by a cleaver is a very painful experience when your hand is protected with a chain glove but catastrophic when not thus protected! While discussing cleavers, it's a good time to mention tables. Going hammer and tong with a cleaver on the kitchen table might be somewhat counterproductive. Be sure your table is up to the punishment you give it – even gentler cutting – and always use the appropriate cutting board. Buy a good thick one (use a red for raw meat, yellow for cooked meat), rather than a thin one, and make sure it is always sterilised before use.

Sterilising items such as cutting boards can be done in many ways. I tend to rub salt into the surface and then rinse it off with a kettle of boiling water. However, you can use a sterilising solution and rinse with cooled boiled water if you prefer.

Of all the knives you can buy, I find that I can get along with the following:

- Slicing knife
- Butcher's knife
- Boning knife

Probably the one I use most is the boning knife, and my steel is in almost constant use.

Using a knife
The best, safest and most efficient way to use a culinary knife is to place it on the surface with the handle pointing towards you. (Never point the blade towards you – which might sound obvious, but people often 'cut round corners', especially when boning, and end up with the blade pointing in awkward positions. Then draw the knife handle towards you so you are cutting on the backstroke. All knives work in this manner unless serrated, but this is only the case with a slicing knife, when you can use a forward stroke too. With a slicing knife, always start

with a backstroke and avoid using a sawing action. Each stroke is deliberate and separate from the previous one.

It goes without saying that you should keep your fingers out of the way!

Mixers and food processors
It is an obvious help to use a power machine, and these days so many of us have them in the kitchen. However, it is possible to complete all the methods described in this book with a knife. In fact, Queen Victoria would only eat sausages made with a knife and not a grinder, but it is a lot slower. The majority of the charcuterie in this book does not call for meat to be pasted. My previous book, *How To Make Your Own Sausages*, deals specifically with sausages from around the world. However, there are some general rules below that will help.

Motors
Less expensive kitchen mixers/processors often have poor motors that do not work well for prolonged periods. The more expensive you get, usually the better the motor.

Pulse
Your machine should have a good pulse action, allowing you to turn it on for a second or two and then off just as easily. From time to time I use ice with meat, particularly in sausage making, but often with pâté too, and the ability to pulse means I do not wreck the blade or the motor.

Sausage attachment
Often, especially with equipment coming from the Far East, the attachments are not standard, and therefore more difficult to source replacements. This is particularly true of sausage stuffers, where I have often had the situation where the stuffers that came with the machine did not even fit properly. Where possible, ask for machines that have Kenwood-type sausage attachments.

Grinders, the old-fashioned hand-cranked type, are

inexpensive and easy to use. They have one drawback, however, and this is to do with the fixing, which is usually a 'G' clamp affair. Often modern worktops do not allow them to fix easily because the amount of screw available is too small to fit, so check your worktops before you buy. There are a number of perfectly adequate sucker-type grinders that will fit anywhere.

Moulds and presses

For many years I made pressed chicken, pressed ham and spam in a glass bowl with a saucer on the top and a few weights added on top of that. Alternatively, I have made sandwich meats – corned beef, mostly – in a loaf tin, with another on top pressing it down, filled with boiling water. However, there comes a time when one wants to make a professional-looking piece of ham in one of those Dutch presses (a wooden affair with a pressing plate attached to a small beam on which you hang weights to increase the pressure), or almost any other shape for that matter, and for this you need an oven press. Spring-loaded and made of metal, they can be acquired fairly cheaply these days secondhand, although you should make sure there is no corrosion inside the mould.

There are many other presses available on the market, with multiple uses. For example, I use one for making cheese and sandwich meat – but not at the same time!

Drying

Essentially, most drying takes place naturally and without any artificial aids at all. I have a drying box; some call it a meat safe. Often it is placed in a sheltered spot outside, but the shed is also a favourite spot. Mine is a big wooden box, about 75cm in all directions, and the four sides are walled with very fine mesh. It has a roof and bottom. Some have humidity and temperature controls, which you can buy separately to enhance a homemade box.

Drying machines

These are not used for drying large pieces of meat. They are superb for slowly drying herbs and making herbal teas from garden leaves. They come in a variety of shapes, but essentially they all work on the same principle. A fan draws warmed air through a series of trays; some are rectangular and others are circular. In a way they resemble a very low-powered hairdryer. I always use mine on its lowest setting.

One of my sons is an Olympic weightlifter and the amount of meat he consumes is phenomenal. Consequently there are always two products in preparation in our kitchen. One of these is dry-cure bacon, and the other is biltong, for which I use my dryer. It takes about three days to completely dry out – and about ten minutes for him to eat it!

Vacuum sealing

This is the process of increasing the shelf life – by a good week in most cases – using a heat-sealed plastic bag. The idea is to stop oxygen from coming ito contact with the meat, which helps keep it fresh. However, this is not the way charcuterie aficionados use vacuum sealers. In this case a piece of meat, salted with the cure, is placed in the plastic vacuum sealing bag and then the machine pumps out the air and makes an airtight (and liquid-tight) seal across the top. This is then placed in the fridge to cure. As liquid is drawn from the meat it is massaged through the plastic bag to ensure the whole surface is covered.

Vacuum sealing is a good way of curing without the mess, and is much more efficient than the pop-it-in-a-plastic-box method.

Scales

A good set of scales is essential – actually two sets are better than one. I have a large scale for weighing big pieces of meat, and a smaller one for weighing out amounts of cure ingredient. Sometimes I try to use my small one for everything, but balancing a piece of meat in such a way that I can see the readout makes the process very difficult. In the past I have lost some to the dog – it having fallen off altogether after being precariously balanced.

When making your own cured meats, you will need to be able to weigh small amounts to an accuracy of 1g (larger pieces of meat require less accuracy). A good 'tare' button is useful, where you put a bowl on the scale and set the readout to zero – saves on the maths!

Meat slicer
These are not cheap bits of kit, but so many bacon makers own a meat slicer because they make perfect slices. To me they are more trouble than any other piece of equipment when it comes to cleaning down, and the rotating blade scares me to death, but there is something about seeing that slice of beautifully cured bacon as it falls onto the back shelf. I also use my meat slicer for slicing pieces of brisket to make biltong, where everything remains even and looks the same.

Of course you could simply use a slicing knife and save yourself a lot of expense.

Pestle and mortar
You cannot get by without these, really. I use mine for crushing and grinding and of course mixing cures. A big rock-based one is often best. The mortar is the bowl, while the pestle is the tool you bash away with, though modesty forbids my mentioning its true etymology. Being metal, you can pound away and put it in the freezer in advance for cold-sensitive recipes.

Sundries
As I have said, it is possible to make all kinds of charcuterie without much in the way of materials, but some just make life easier. A good supply of muslin (cheesecloth) is essential. I use them to dry hams, etc. Wrap the meat loosely in a piece of muslin and then place another over the top of this and secure into position with butcher's twine. This keeps the insect world off your produce and allows the meat to dry slowly.

Butcher's hooks are a godsend. You can use them for so many things, as well as hanging meat and sausages. They are good for draining cheeses and drying/storing vegetables. Believe me, it is much easier hooking a butcher's hook than tying a knot in a piece of string with your arms in the air!

Essentially nylon and quite strong, nets are a simple way to place a joint that you want to keep in a particular shape. However, they are not intended to be used as a way of keeping insects out of food – the gaps are too big.

Brine pumps are useful if you are wet curing a ham that is on the large size, i.e. more than about 10cm deep. You put cure solution into the pump and inject it into the centre of the meat. The ham is then wet cured in the usual manner (see page 22).

An excellent meat thermometer, preferably a digital one, is a must for cooking joints, hot smoking bacon and hams, etc. This is a must-have piece of equipment. It's a good idea to calibrate it regularly with boiling water just so you know you are getting the correct reading. To calibrate your thermometer, simply place the measuring prong in some boiling water. It should read more or less 100°C or 212°F.

As I have already mentioned, clothing is an essential part of your cleanliness regime. I wear large aprons, and since I have little hair, I don't worry too much about a hat! If you tend to drop your mop at regular intervals, you should wear a good hair restraint, however. This could be a butcher's hat, with your hair tucked into the cavity, a hairnet (available in packs of twelve from butcher's suppliers on the internet) or even a shower cap if you can stand looking a little silly! Many people wear neoprene gloves (which come in boxes of 100) and these can be useful, especially when massaging paprika where the skin tends to discolour quite rapidly and can take a long time to wear off. If you have a sensitive skin when it comes to salt, you will find them essential.

Chemicals used in curing

It seems odd to espouse a product that is at the same time wholesome and good but has various chemicals added to it. However, no traditional bacon or ham making takes place without salt – and to a large extent sugar too!

Salt

There is a lot of discussion in this book about salt and what sort to use. It has to be said that the influence of European curing and American processes are all around, and as you will inevitably look on the internet for recipes, you will find a huge amount of conflicting information. This book contains recipes that have worked for me, and continue to work. But everyone is responsible for what they consume, so always be happy with what you are doing.

Nowhere is this more important than in the matter of salt, which after all is the main curing agent for hams and bacon, etc. Ordinary salt, sea salt, kosher salt and even kitchen table salt (though I would discourage its use) preserve in most cases. However, the dreaded *Clostridium botulinum*, the little perisher that causes botulism, can 'get through the net' as it were. Consequently other substances are added, such as saltpetre. This is sold as Pink salt, or Prague powder, and there are two versions of it: #1 and #2. Pink salt and #1 are fundamentally the same, containing potassium nitrate. Prague powder #2 has potassium nitrite added. These products are added in small quantities to your main salt to keep botulism at bay. End of story. Except that the UK has a generally different product called curing salt. This is a salt made up of ordinary salt and the right amount of potassium nitrate and nitrite to give a safe product. In this case the salt is not dyed pink and it is used instead of most combinations – most of the recipes in this book use it.

Potassium nitrite is used where the product is eaten raw, and also where the meat is so large, it is difficult to get enough salt *in situ*. One thing about these additional salts is that they do add flavour and they make the meat a pleasing pink colour too.

Always keep your salt in an airtight container. It draws water from the atmosphere, which is fine if you are using an excess of salt, but if you are weighing out a specific amount then the water in the salt will affect your quantities.

You will find more on these salts in the appropriate chapters.

Sugar

Often used in curing pork products, particularly bacon and ham. Lots of variations are used in the sugars, and whereas sugar is useful for a small amount of preserving – hence its use in jams – curing meat takes some of its flavour as a priority. All kinds of sugars are popular, from maple syrup, molasses, honey and any number of brown unrefined sugars to ordinary refined white sugar.

I like to keep sugar for curing separately from the other sugars in the kitchen, just in case I cross-contaminate it, and where possible I store it in an airtight container too.

Herbs and spices

I tend to keep coriander seeds, black pepper, cloves, garlic, bay leaves, lovage, mint and mustard powder for most of my curing purposes. The coriander is used mostly in biltong preparation, and black peppercorns are kept for almost everything. Mostly I use fresh, though I do dry herbs from the garden, especially for curing.

I never use products such as garlic salt or onion powder. If I want an onion flavour, I use onion. Lots of recipes, mostly from the US, call for onion powder or onion salt, but I don't like the artificial flavour. To be honest, I have never been that interested in creating layers of strong flavours and I consider the hams, bacon and cured products I make to be largely ingredients whose flavours should come to the fore. I don't like to spoil them by adding all kinds of flavours. Consequently, paprika is not on my list – though I keep it in the kitchen, and if I see a recipe that calls for paprika, I always think twice about it.

Vinegar

This is an important preserving material, and many pickles are kept in vinegar. On the whole it is mostly used as an antiseptic, particularly for wiping fungal growths from the surface of meat and dip-sterilising wooden skewers before doing a smell test of hams (see also page 65).

I use malt vinegar more often than anything else, but many others such as cider vinegar or red wine vinegar are equally good.

Salt liquids

I keep two products for flavour and preserving. The first is Worcestershire sauce, with which I make biltong (see also page 96). It is multi-functional. Firstly the salt content augments the sea salt I add to the meat. It flavours the meat and acts as a glue for the coriander seeds that I sprinkle over the meat.

The same goes for soy sauce, which makes a great addition to a wet-cure bacon with a hint of China!

The bare minimum

When it comes down to it, the only things you need to get started on curing your own bacon and ham are a good knife, a lidded heatproof plastic container for easy sterilisation and cleaning (place your meat inside while it is curing) and salt, plus a little sugar for flavour. However, you will soon be adding mustard and black pepper to your bacon. Note: you could use a lidded casserole or even a large bowl plus clingfilm to seal during the curing process in place of the plastic container. Also ensure that your starters list includes some cleansing and sterilising equipment as well as protective clothing. You really can, and I did for many years, get on perfectly well with just this equipment. The rest will come as you get bitten by the bug, or perhaps as people congratulate you on your prowess.

Eventually you will need a whole room to store the equipment you have purchased. Some items may be used only once or twice, while others will become inseparable companions on your culinary adventures.

Chapter 2

Introduction to bacon and ham

Perhaps the most encouraging start to any curing hobby is to make your own bacon. The results are usually such an improvement on supermarket products that the possibilities of future triumphs ignite the imagination, and almost at once you are planning your next batch. What can I add? What to leave out, a tweak here, a modification there. And often, 'How can I make such and such?' Memories of amazing dishes enjoyed years ago rise up to tempt us.

Bacon and its European relatives originated in small farms. It was peasant food, borne of necessity. A pig can be consumed in a week – cooked, roasted, made into soup or sliced – but cured pig lasts much longer. You don't need to scoff the lot! Essentially salted pork is salted pork. It is much the same throughout the world, but there are differences from product to product, country to country, and even from town to town. The gastronomy of the pig-eating peoples of the world is one of subtlety, of plenty and great delight.

Discover the difference between bacon, pancetta, prosciutto and ham below!

Bacon: how it is made and used

Traditionally bacon is made from the belly of the pig in Europe and America, though in the UK it is also frequently made from loin with a smaller piece of belly on the end, giving it the traditional 'rasher' shape. It is lightly cured with salt and sugar, sometimes with other flavours added, such as mustard powder, herbs and pepper.

Often bacon is also cold-smoked, more so a hundred years ago in the UK than today. The smoking process was to improve the keeping qualities, and it obviously added to the flavour. Cold smoking, as we shall see elsewhere in this book, does not increase the temperature of the meat and therefore it remains uncooked.

Bacon was traditionally hung in cool larders and cellars. Used as required, it was kept in muslin, with lard rubbed into the cloth to keep flies off the meat. As soon as refrigeration became widespread in the 1930s (although it was not until the 1960s that freezers became popular in the domestic home), butchers would keep cold rooms where bacon could be stored and sliced on demand for customers. Efficient as this system may have been, a side of bacon, known as a 'flitch', would serve a large number of people and therefore not be hanging around for long periods. Home bacon making, meanwhile, saw a sad decline. Eventually, bacon as we know it was sold ready-sliced in plastic packets, invisibly protected with chemicals, and any notion of patina and quality left to be guessed at by judging the price. More or less ubiquitously around the world, save for the UK, where both smoked and unsmoked varieties are popular, bacon is smoked and cooked as a part of the process, to be cooked again at home – a crispy, almost burnt atom of flavour used more as a condiment than an ingredient in a meal. Save for the UK, the bacon butty has hardly any place around the world.

Being lightly cured, usually for short periods, bacon should always be cooked.

Pancetta: how it is made and used

This is an Italian version of bacon, lightly cured (often only with salt), though some other flavours are added, including regional herbs such as sage plus salt and sugar. Mustard and black pepper are often used too. It is almost always made from pork belly and is sliced very thinly or cut into small cubes to add to various dishes. Unlike bacon, which is consumed more or less on its own merit, pancetta is usually used to flavour more complex dishes such as baked salmon or white fish where the pancetta is fried separately then mixed with tomato and oregano to serve as an accompanying sauce.

Like bacon, pancetta should always be cooked. This is an important point because people tend to misinterpret the country of origin of pancetta and automatically assume that it is edible raw.

Pancheta adobada is a Spanish version of pancetta flavoured with garlic and paprika, with regional variations in France. Ventreche is a French version, smoked and very lightly cured. The cure is simply salt, black pepper and smoke! An unsmoked variety called petit sale is also available.

When making carbonara sauce, cooks in the UK often replace pancetta with bacon cut into small pieces. This is a real mistake. For a start the average rasher of bacon is much less fatty and the quality of the meat is different thinly sliced rather than in small or even large chunks. Bacon is bacon, whereas pancetta is similar but different.

Recipes for pancetta can be found on page 53.

Prosciutto: how it is made and used

This is the same as ham, but with obvious differences in additional flavours and certain techniques. Literally referring to the hind leg of the pig or the boar, prosciutto is generally translated as ham, and like all hams around the world can be cured and air-dried (prosciutto crudo) or cooked (prosciutto coto). Either way, there is no need for cooking prior to consumption.

The process of making prosciutto can be complex, lengthy and fraught with difficulties. If the working conditions are too warm, too wet or too dry, the product can be ruined, and this is why air-dried hams are particularly popular in southern European countries, where the weather can generally be relied on to create the right conditions, unlike in northern countries, where it is very humid and often extremely variable in temperature. You get York ham and maybe a few more in the UK, but an endless list from Spain, southern France, Italy, Portugal and the Mediterranean.

Prosciutto is first salted, often for a month, and then washed and dried. During the salting process the meat is often pressed with a board and heavy weights to remove as much blood as possible. It is then hung for a very long time – often more than a year, and eighteen months is not uncommon. Traditionally prosciutto ham is kept in caves to mature, but the drying cabinet

– a temperature- and humidity-controlled cupboard – has made it possible for prosciutto to be made more or less anywhere.

Paolo Arrigo, an Italian and managing director of Seeds of Italy, opened my eyes to the food of Italy. As with seeds, so with food. We were discussing the similarity between Italian vegetables and British ones. I wondered why this would be the case when Italy is so much hotter than the UK. And how is it that Italian food tastes so different to British cuisine? Paolo pointed out that the key to growing Italian vegetables was the mountains; most of the food was not grown in the valleys, which was kept for rice and wheat, olives and grapes, but everything else was grown a thousand or so metres up, where it was much more temperate. Moreover, it was all kept as simple as possible. No special techniques: just sunshine, water and maybe, if it was available, fertiliser. The same went for Italian cooking. Naturally there were certain combinations of flavours archetypal to the cuisine. The use of olive oil, basil and garlic, for example, though not in such quantities to smother the flavour of the produce. And that is our mistake: in the UK we add too much, and do not rely on the natural flavours of the food.

Nowhere is this more relevant than in the world of home curing, where we add all kinds of flavour because we think we ought, but in truth it is not necessary. Prosciutto is simply prepared, frequently even without sugar or any aromatic flavours added. The addition of aromatics came from the need to keep insects off the meat while it was drying, and a slurry of salted rosemary, garlic, bay, basil and lavender was used to cover the meat until the outer surface became impenetrable by drying.

Prosciutto is served thinly sliced and can be eaten uncooked. It is often cooked in pasta dishes or used on pizzas but more frequently appears as a tapas dish.

Ham: how it is made and used

What we tend to call ham in the UK comes in two forms: ham and gammon. Generally the difference between the two is that gammon is sold raw and needs to be cooked. Ham is either cooked or air-dried and is therefore ready to eat without cooking.

Ham destined for cooking and gammons are cured for a shorter period, usually wet cured. In wet curing, salt penetrates the meat more evenly, and it is usual for some of the cure to be injected directly into the muscle – otherwise the thickness of the meat might be such that insufficient salt reaches the centre during the week or so of curing. Such short curing times compared to those of air-dried hams necessitate cooking, which is usually roasting or boiling for ham (or a combination of boiling and roasting), and gammon is frequently thickly sliced and then fried like bacon. Some people prefer gammon to bacon because it has much less fat.

Hams are often smoked, usually under oak or apple, but there are many variations. Westphalia hams are smoked with a combination of oak and juniper wood. Juniper is a resinous wood with a pine fragrance, making the Westphalia ham the exception that proves the rule – don't smoke with pine!

In many countries, Spain particularly, hams are so revered that they fetch astronomical prices. The basic ham is jamón serrano. It is from the mountains and is produced from white landrace pigs, the animals being fed in many ways – often with acorns, but with commercial feed too. However, jamón iberico is priced differently according to what the animals have been fed on! These can fetch hundreds of pounds a ham, a little like Japanese wagyu beef, but with less massaging involved!

Recipes for cures

You will find, as you delve into the world of curing ham and making bacon in all its forms, that the amount of salt used varies enormously. Obviously, the amount of salt used in a wet cure may well be very different to the dry-cure equivalent – some people use cure at 5 per cent of the weight of meat, others 15 per cent and still more at 25 per cent. It takes some time to find your favourite recipes and the amount of salt you feel happy with, and consequently when you start curing hams and bacon it is always something of an experiment.

Dry cures
For a wet cure I tend to make a brine containing 400g curing salt to 4 litres of water, and any other flavours are additional to this. This gives me a 9 per cent salt-to-water cure. However, for dry cures I use about 35g curing salt per kilo of meat, which is much less salt but more of it gets in!

As a general rule, use a 5 per cent dry cure (that is, 5 per cent of the weight of the meat as curing salt) to start with and check the saltiness to see if it is to your taste. You can then amend all recipes accordingly. One of the best things I ever did was to keep a notebook of my various attempts, right down to the very last detail, and, of course, what the taste was like! I found I could refer to it time and again – sometimes various combinations of flavours didn't work well for me, and the relative combinations of flavours can make a difference too, but it's amazing how easy it is to forget how much you added of this and that, so a notebook is quite possibly the most important piece of equipment you will need.

This book details specific recipes. You can compare the basic cures with those found in this chapter, and by all means amend them. The reason why there are so many different recipes for cures out there is precisely because curing is basically a simple task and people make up their own cures, write them down as recipes, and that's that.

Following American recipes
You will see that most, if not all, American and Continental European recipes usually call for kosher salt and pink salt (and we have discussed this a lot in this book). Some recipes you will come across call for the addition of Prague powder, #1 or #2. Here, we are concentrating on a product in the UK that is often called curing salts and marketed as Supacure. This product contains ordinary salt with nitrite and nitrate which when rubbed in at the rate of 15 per cent of the meat weight gives exactly the legal permitted amount of nitrite and nitrate in the product. It contains 97 per cent salt, 2 per cent potassium nitrate E252 and 1 per cent sodium nitrite E250.

In order to follow a recipe that calls for Prague powder or pink salt, simply use Supacure in the following manner. This recipe provides a basic cure per kilo of meat:

22.5g salt
8g sugar
2.5g cure #1

Note the 2.5g cure #1 and 22.5g salt. Simply add the two weights together and use that amount of Supacure curing salt.

So, it becomes:

25g curing salt
8g sugar

Although there doesn't seem to be that much flavour in there, it will make great bacon!

Wet cure

The basis of a wet cure is to make a brine with appropriate flavourings, the meat being soaked in the brine for a specific period of time. Here, the pork doesn't lose much water in the process, but the salt and flavours leach from the cure solution and into the meat. For this reason, the skin is usually removed from the joint prior to curing and it is important that the meat is regularly turned to ensure an even soak. For larger pieces of meat, some of the cure is injected into the meat using what resembles an horrific Victorian medical syringe.

Wet cure hams have to be cooked, and are the mainstay of boiled and roast hams. It has become popular in the US and elsewhere to hot-smoke hams in a temperature-controlled smoker at low-ish temperature for most of the smoking cycle, then increase the heat to ensure proper cooking.

The amount of salt used in the cure (some people call it a 'pickle', but I think pickles have vinegar) varies enormously. Some recipes use a kilo of curing salt per 4.5 litres of cure. They ask for the meat to be 'stabbed' through to the bone with a skewer or knife to allow the cure easier access to the meat. Other recipes use much less salt overall and call for a specific amount to be injected into the meat. Whichever recipe you choose, it is important to move the meat around. Floating hams in food-grade buckets will need to be weighed down with a board, so the whole ham is submerged and turned around daily. Note: food-grade buckets specially made to hold food are easily cleaned and resistant to bleach and boiling water. Often they will hold 10 litres of liquid or more, but they can be smaller and usually come with a lid. Increasingly popular are sealable plastic curing bags – the cure and meat are added and the bag sealed, having had all the air excluded, so there is no real chance of the meat being exposed to the air. Normally, the process of curing hams takes place over ten days.

Wet cure bacon is a very similar process and was introduced to the UK with the invention of the Wiltshire cure, which is thought to have been in the eighteenth century. It revolutionised the way we eat bacon. Wiltshire was renowned for its pigs, and whereas the poor of the county could eat only the offal and maybe some cuts such as hog's face, ear and trotters, the rich had the joints and the bacon.

Wiltshire cure was originally a dry cure. The Harris family found their cold cellars made it possible to create a bacon with less cure, and even though it didn't last too long in warm weather (around a couple of weeks), it was cheaper. Further economies were found by the replenishing of salt in spent wet cure, which still had the remnants of cure from the previous batch. It soon became possible for ordinary people to buy bacon from time to time as a special treat. The product was sold by butchers, used as required, and consequently in the average urban household at least bacon was a cured meat bought especially for a meal or two. We still eat bacon like this today, often wrapped in plastic with some greasy, fat- and chemical-laden cure in the wrapper!

Injecting cure

This process is a part of wet curing ham, and other meats for that matter. Essentially the cure is injected into the muscle using what looks like a desperately large hypodermic syringe and the whole ham is simultaneously dunked in brine solution. The reason for this is because of the depth of muscle and how far the salt has to penetrate that muscle. There will be a gradient of salt concentration that is highest at the outer portion of the meat and diminishes as you go further in, but if you add cure directly to the centre of the meat then an equilibrium of salt concentration is achieved more easily.

Using honey or syrup in curing

There are lots of recipes for cures containing honey, molasses or even treacle. Almost all of them also have sugar added to the cure. Personally, I prefer to separate the liquid sugar from the rest of the cure because I feel it inhibits the penetration of salt.

Many people use a honey cure in a curing bag, so eventually the salt will penetrate – helped by it dissolving in the liquor from the meat. When making a recipe, I tend to leave out the honey and then add it later for a few days as a separate process.

I am rather fussy about the type of honey used in curing. I'm not impressed with plastic squeezy bottles of honey because they are usually boiled and treated to make them pour more easily and you simply cannot get the real honey flavour. Actually I prefer set honey, which is spread over the cured bacon with a knife. However, local honey is just as good. You simply would not credit the difference between honey sourced from a local hive and that bought from the supermarket – the flavours are so much better.

Chapter 3

Bacon curing

It is strange to find out about your television heroes and realise they were not always what you thought them to be. It wasn't until many years after being transfixed by Jack Hargreaves' *Out Of Town* series of programmes on Southern Television – all about the bygone days of country life – while researching to write his biography and found that whereas he was a brilliant communicator, and possibly the most knowledgeable person in the UK on country ways, some of the things he said needed a pinch of salt! So it was with bacon and eggs. Jack banged on about bacon and eggs being the British national dish. He believed this was the case because most people with a bit of room to spare kept a pig and some hens. Clearly he never knew 'up north' where he claimed to have come from, where all the pigs belonged to the nearest abbey and all the rest of the people had to make do with the blood and some of the offal. Black pudding and eggs would have been nearer the mark! Anyway, the 'full English' might be thought of as the national dish, or indeed the full Welsh, or the full Scottish, or whichever hotel you happen to be staying in, but there are many contenders for the national dish prize, including the ubiquitous chicken tikka.

Actually, making bacon is relatively easy and there are so many recipes out there so there is always something to try regardless of your skill level. The most important thing is to keep everything completely clean and sterilised (see also page 7) and don't go crazy with the added flavours first time around – just keep it simple.

Bacon: how it is made and used
When making bacon, it is important to remember the following:

- Different recipes call for different levels of salt
- Bacon makers have their own ideas about what is salty or not, so don't be afraid to adjust a recipe to your taste

- Don't keep bacon in warm conditions; always refrigerate it
- Sealable bags are excellent for curing and keeping bacon
- Resist the temptation to simply store bacon in the cure – it won't keep it any longer
- An extra day in the cure will not make bacon much saltier
- A little extra salt will hardly be noticed
- Skin and fat do not allow salt to permeate too deeply.

Essentially, what we are doing here is salting pork. Originally, this process was to help prevent the pork from going off, but these days it is more about flavour. When it comes to how much salt to use, you will find a huge variation in recommendations. This is quite a puzzle to the new curer because it is confusing to see someone making bacon with 50g salt per kilo while others use 22g salt per kilo.

There are a number of important points to bear in mind when it comes to using cures:

- For the vast majority of meat curing, it is salt that makes everything safe so don't try to get rid of it altogether
- A little extra salt will hardly be noticed in your bacon. A cure with 37g salt per kilo will not be any saltier than one with 32g salt per kilo
- Similarly, an extra day in the cure will not make a lot of difference to the saltiness of your bacon
- Finally, and importantly, a period of at least a day, and preferably two, out of the cure allows the salt to equalise throughout the meat.

Bacon recipes
First-ever 'easy' bacon
The basic process includes buying pork, slicing the pork as if it was bacon, mixing the cure, sprinkling the cure over the meat, which is placed on a tray, piling the 'rashers', wrapping them in clingfilm and refrigerating overnight. This method of making bacon comes with a bit of a twist. It doesn't create a product that

will last a month, although you can vacuum seal and keep in the fridge, which means it will last a little longer than a few days, probably about ten. We never keep ours long enough to find out – it has always been very quickly polished off! But more importantly, it turns all the ideas about amounts of salt on their head, which just goes to show how arbitrary much of the process is. The idea came about to overcome a number of problems in an easy manner, making it easy to create bacon and having a measured amount of salt in the product.

The home curing method, wet or dry, leaves you with a product where it is really difficult to tell how much salt is in it in the normal everyday kitchen. The problem is you need a lot of salt on the outside of the pork for it to penetrate to the centre of the meat. A large piece of meat can have cure injected into it, but there is an easier way.

In order to get to the centre of the cut of meat you can either inject, as described earlier on page 24, or simply slice the meat before it is cured. In slicing pork as though it is already cured (already bacon), you have access to the cut surface of each slice so it is possible to make a cure that is only 1 per cent of the meat weight and to be sure that all the cure gets solely where it is needed.

You need 10g curing salt per kilo of pork. Add to this an equal amount of sugar – I prefer golden sugar, but plain white will do.

1. In a bowl, mix together the ingredients really well. You could add other flavours if you like – the world is your oyster – but the first time you do this, use only the cure mix so you can judge how well seasoned it is for you. (I have used oyster sauce, chilli sauce or flakes, mustard powder, black pepper, sage and curry powder – the list goes goes on. Sprinkle the cure mix first and then the flavourings.)

2. Now slice your pork into rashers and arrange on a baking sheet or a roasting tin (it needn't be deep). Simply sprinkle the

rashers evenly with the cure mix so that each slice gets a similar amount of cure.

3. Pile the rashers on top of each other so you have layers. Wrap in clingfilm, or stack in a lidded polythene box. Remember, the lowest slice will have a surface with no cure on it, so add a little to this in the wrapping.

4. Place in the fridge overnight and you will have great, dry cured bacon.

Note: If 10g salt is not quite tasty enough for you, try using 15g per kilo and then decreasing it the next time. Remember to always use the same quantity of sugar, though.

You will find this bacon leaks liquid as all cured products do. This should be poured off, but there won't be copious amounts. In cooking, the bacon does not poach, unlike injected supermarket bacon, and it will not shrink or leave a white fatty congealed mess behind. Furthermore the flavour is quite literally wonderful!

If you cannot slice the pork yourself, ask your butcher to do this for you. He will probably want to know why you are doing it, and he might poke fun at you, but you can always take him a bacon sandwich!

You can cut down the amount of sugar once you are used to it. This is particularly useful if your bacon is caramelising too much and leaving black carbon in your pan.

Now you might ask: is this a legitimate way of making bacon? Surely this is just heavy seasoning? Well, it's not! The meat will last ten days in the fridge. More importantly, would I be wrong in preferring this bacon to the plastic-wrapped, wet, chemical-laden stuff to be found on the supermarket shelf? The only thing I can say is this: as a staple bacon recipe it is easy, cheap and marvellous. Give it a try!

This bacon is really good hot or cold smoked. It often seems to be too much fuss to prepare hot smoking for just a kilo of bacon rashers and so I invented the beekeeper's smoker version of smoking bacon just for this (see page 177). It takes about ten applications to get a good smoky flavour, which is a couple of hours in total.

How to test whether the bacon is cured

Curers are worriers. They, myself included, have an aversion to producing bad or unhealthy products, and so I always check the state of the cure when I think it should have finished.

- Remove the meat from the cure and give it a quick rinse under cold running water. It should feel distinctly hard and be a dark pink colour.
- Now cut a piece in half and inspect the cut surface. It should be uniformly hard and pink. If not, soak it for another couple of days. The only time when bacon might not be fully cured in the centre is if the meat is more than 5–7cm thick.
- For a wet cure you might need up to ten days to fully cure a thick piece of pork. In this case, consider injecting cure with a meat syringe (available online). Usually I find pork loin takes a lot longer than pork belly for obvious reasons – the belly is a much thinner joint.

Wet cured bacon

Buying bacon at the supermarket is not simply a way of getting meat for the table. It educates us too, in a way the supermarket, and the bacon producers, prefer. For example, we are led to believe that wet cure bacon is somehow cheaper than dry cure simply because that is our experience. We are also led to believe that wet cure bacon actually produces a messy deposit in the pan and the meat doesn't actually fry, it poaches in its own chemical-laden mess.

Of course, cheap bacon is always going to be of a lower quality, but that doesn't mean homemade wet cure bacon has to be of inferior quality too. The main reason for making a wet cure is flavour. Wonderful flavours can be introduced more easily into your meat by using a wet cure. In particular, I am thinking about beer-cured bacon (see page 30), but there are many more possibilities.

Everyday wet cured bacon

This is the basic cure for bacon with no real flavour enhancements, but you can easily alter it to create all kinds of masterpieces.

For a kilo of pork belly you will need: 400g curing salt, 200g brown sugar and 4 litres water.

1. First, remove the skin and any bones from the pork belly. Removing the skin is easy with a sharp paring or filleting knife. Make a cut just beneath the skin and pull back with your fingers, making long cuts to release the skin as you go along. Note: it is not always necessary to remove the skin but essential if you want your bacon rind-free. To remove the spare ribs, locate them with your fingers and cut between each rib, following the edge. You will find the top of any bones, which you can then trim out. Cut any ragged meat away to give a clean finish. Of course you can ask your butcher to do this for you too.

2. Place all the ingredients except the pork in a large pan and cover with water. Bring to the boil and then allow it to cool.

3. Once cooled, immerse the pork in the brine and cover with at least 3cm of it. Cover (you may need to weigh it down to make sure the meat is submerged) and place in the fridge for seven days. Turn the meat over every day.

4. The meat should be noticeably harder and brown in colour. Remove, rinse under the tap and then slice thinly, according to how you like your bacon.

This is a simple bacon, but extraordinarily tasty, and it is easy to enhance. Try exchanging some of the water for apple juice or dark beer. A tablespoon of mustard powder, peppercorns, juniper berries or honey is also good.

Maple wet cured bacon

This is the basic bacon recipe that you can use as a starting point for all kinds of experimentation. The cure flavours can be amended, as required. It will produce about 700g of bacon. Sometimes referred to as Canadian bacon, it is frequently made from pork loin. The resting process is an important one. It allows the salt to pervade the meat equally.

1kg pork belly, boned (see page 30, or your butcher can do this for you)
400g curing salt
10g crushed peppercorns
1 onion, sliced
Handful of rosemary
6 garlic cloves, sliced
300ml maple syrup
4 litres water

1. To make the brine, place all the ingredients (except the meat) in a large pan and bring to the boil for 10 minutes. Strain off any scum that appears and pass through muslin into a heatproof glass bowl to cool.

2. Remove the skin from the meat and as much fat as you prefer.

3. Once cooled, transfer the cure to a plastic container and then pour the cure over the meat. It needs to be about 3cm higher than the meat, which is then weighed down with a plate. Place in the fridge.

4. Turn the meat over each day for seven days and then remove from the cure, wash and pat dry with a clean tea towel or kitchen paper towels.

5. Return the meat to the fridge on a covered plate for a day or so and then slice for cooking. Alternatively, you can smoke the meat prior to cooking (see Chapter 12 for detailed instructions).

Garlic pickle bacon

This is a lovely recipe that produces a bacon with hints of garlic since the brine is more cooked than simply sloshed together. For a kilo of pork belly, you will need the following:

400g curing salt
1 tsp peppercorns
4 bruised bay leaves (rub and scrunch them in your hands)
1 onion, quartered
5 garlic cloves, crushed and chopped
200g brown sugar (or try 200ml honey or maple syrup)
4 litres water

1. First, remove the skin from the pork belly and any bones (see page 30).

2. Place all the ingredients (except the pork and water) in a large pan and cover with the water. Bring to the boil and simmer for 20 minutes. Sieve the liquid into a heatproof container and allow to cool.

3. Once cooled, immerse the pork in the pickling mixture and cover with at least 3cm of pickle. Cover (you might also need to weigh it down with a small plate to submerge the meat) and place in the fridge for seven days. Turn the meat over every day.

4. The meat should be noticeably harder and browned in colour. Remove, rinse under the tap and then slice as bacon.

Dry cured bacon

Solid and full of flavour, dry cured bacon has long been regarded as the best. Most importantly, it is fascinating to make at home. It is created by the rub-in method – that is, you make the cure and rub it into your meat then leave it to weep. The salt draws water from the meat as it travels inward. As the liquid seeps from the meat, the salt is dissolved, creating a brine. Do not remove this liquid: it is acting as a buffer, equalising the salt concentration in the developing bacon.

Most people start off with a 5 per cent salt cure – that is, of the weight of meat, you need 5 per cent of the cure to be salt. Over the years I have chosen to reduce this for my own consumption to 3.7 per cent salt, so for every kilo I use 37g salt, plus whatever else I wish to add.

You can easily alter the recipes to 5 per cent to discover how much you personally prefer, remembering of course not to reduce it by too much if you are going to keep the bacon for a few weeks.

Everyday dry cure bacon

I make this recipe every week as our family of five adults consumes about 750g, so there is always some on the go. On the whole I use pork loin, and every few weeks choose a belly joint.

1 slab of pork, skinned and boned (see page 30, or your butcher can do this for you)
Per kilo of meat:
37g curing salt
20g good dark sugar
1g crushed black pepper

1. First, mix together the dry ingredients in a bowl and then sprinkle evenly over the meat. Rub in with your fingertips.

2. Place in a lidded plastic box and keep in the fridge to cure. Turn the meat every day for six days, spooning any crystals and liquid over the meat (you will notice the liquid seeping out of the meat). You can check the cure state by slicing the bacon in two. Look at the cut surface and you should have a completely uniform cure, where the meat is darker and firmer. Any softness and pinkness in the centre means the meat is not completely cured and it will need another couple of days of curing.

3. After the curing time, remove and wash the bacon, rinse out the box and pat everything dry with a clean tea towel or kitchen paper towels. Refrigerate for another two days – or longer, if you like – with the lid off to help the meat dry a little. This is an important part of the process, allowing the salt in the meat to equalise. Then you can slice your bacon accordingly.

Jalapeño bacon

There are lots of recipes for this bacon on the internet, and it's hardly surprising to find they are mostly from the United States. The Americans have a different take on bacon, often curing, then baking, and finally frying it. The result is a crispy product, which is brittle and easily sprinkled. Here is a recipe I have modified and found to work really well. In this case it is important, I think, to follow the American tradition and to bake before frying. The whole piece of pork is baked and then sliced for frying, as required.

1 slab of pork, skinned and boned
(see page 30, or your butcher can do this for you)
Per kilo of meat:
37g curing salt
20g good dark sugar
1g crushed black pepper
4 pickled jalapeños
4 garlic cloves, crushed

1. This is a two-part process. First, the dry ingredients are mixed together in a bowl and sprinkled evenly over the meat. Then the jalapeños and crushed garlic are blended and spooned over the meat to cover the salted surface.

2. Place in a lidded plastic box and keep in the fridge for six days, turning and redistributing the cure so the meat gets a complete coverage.

3. After the curing time, remove and wash the bacon, rinse out the box and pat everything dry with a clean tea towel or kitchen paper towels. Keep for another two days – or longer if you like, with the lid off, and then you can decide what you will do next, as described in the next step.

4. You can cold smoke the meat for 3 hours or so using applewood as a basis (see Chapter 12, pages 174–76, for detailed

instructions on smoking). Then store for slicing and frying. Alternatively, cover in foil and bake at 180°C (Gas 4) for 40 minutes and allow to cool before slicing and frying.

5. To store, wrap in clingfilm or place in vacuum-sealed packets and refrigerate up to a month (it can also be frozen for up to three months).

Honey bacon (whole in a bag)

There are two ways to do this, but the recipe below calls for a simple all-in approach. Alternatively, you can simply cure the bacon with everything but the honey and then, once cured, cover with honey and leave for a few days to get the same effect.
For a really exotic bacon, cure the bacon without the honey and get your hands on some set honey (preferably from a local beekeeper) and gather some lavender flowers. Place the flowers over the surface of the meat and then smear with a liberal amount of honey.

2 kg piece of pork belly, ribs removed but skin on (see page 30, or ask your butcher to do this for you)
Per kilo of meat use:
37g curing salt
1 tbsp chilli flakes
1 tsp mustard powder
50g honey

1. Wash, dry and weigh the meat and work out the amount of cure you have to use by using 37g salt per kilo.

2. Mix all the dry ingredients together in a bowl and rub all over the meat with your fingertips. Pour over the honey, preferably doing so in a curing bag or a lidded plastic box.

3. Keep in the fridge for a week (do not cover), turning the meat over each day and rubbing the cure into the meat side – even if the skin is uppermost for that day. If your meat is less than 5cm thick it will be ready in a week, otherwise leave it for two more days.

4. Remove from the cure, wash and pat dry with a clean tea towel or kitchen paper towels. Place on a rack in the fridge and leave for two days. It will keep in the fridge for two to three weeks and you can freeze it too in a vacuum-sealed bag or up to three months. You can also smoke the meat – hickory worked well for me (see Chapter 12, pages 174–76, for detailed instructions on smoking).

American hot smoked bacon

This is full of flavours, and the various recipes out there add even more flavours to the product. To be frank, I hardly see the point of a multitude of flavours except if you are using bacon as a condiment, a kind of atom bomb salty and piquant blast, cooked until it is completely crispy and sprinkled on salad. Actually, instead of slicing this bacon into rashers, you can cut it into lardons, cook them until they are crispy and then sprinkle them on almost anything.

The basic idea of American bacon is that it is cooked twice. A fairly incomplete cooking is followed by finishing off in the pan or grill, or indeed using the bacon as an ingredient in another recipe. This accounts for the Americans' love of crispy bacon.

A slab piece of pork belly, ribs removed, skin on
(see page 30, or ask your butcher to do this for you)
Per kilo of meat:
4 garlic cloves
37g curing salt
35g dark brown sugar
1g freshly ground black pepper
1g chilli flakes

1. First, wash the pork and pat dry with a clean towel or kitchen paper towels.

2. Roughly chop the garlic and add to a mixing bowl along with all the cure ingredients; mix well.

3. This bacon is best cured in a sealable bag, although you can use a large plastic container if you wish. However, there is not a great volume of cure, so a bag is better. Make sure all the pork is in contact with the cure.

4. Place the meat in the bag and add the cure. Expel the air and seal – you may need to wrap the bag in lots of clingfilm, but keep a dish to catch any drips. A vacuum sealer is best, or a zip-lock bag.

5. Keep refrigerated for five days, turning each day to maintain an even flow of salt, after which you should be able to remove the meat from the bag, wash, pat dry and leave in the open (but still in the fridge).

6. This bacon is hot smoked, skin face down. If you have a temperature-controlled smoker, set it to 94°C (201°F) and smoke until the internal temperature reaches 65°C (149°F). This should take 2–3 hours. However, I use a barbecue to smoke bacon, with a framework over the barbecue, and apple pellets are added to the charcoal. The barbecue is a lidded one, and I keep the heat as low as possible, building the smoke slowly, taking the temperature with a meat thermometer every 20 minutes or so. Once it has reached 65°C (149°F), I keep it as close to that for about 30 minutes.

7. When the meat is removed from the smoker or barbecue, allow to cool. Clearly the skin will have taken the brunt of the smoke, and will now be very dark. This is why I leave it on for the smoking period, but now I remove it once the meat is sufficiently cool.

Cooking with bacon

What can you do with bacon apart from making good old-fashioned bacon and eggs? Here are some of my favourite recipes. Remember, homemade bacon can be quite salty, so always check the seasoning.

Bacon, Brie and beef tomato toasts
Serves 2

1 beef tomato, cut into 4 thick slices
1–2 tsp balsamic vinegar
4 thick slices of bread
Butter as liked
4 rashers of bacon, grilled
4 wedges Brie
Salt and black pepper to taste

1. Place the tomato slices on a plate and drizzle with balsamic vinegar. Season with a little salt and black pepper if you wish.

2. Toast the bread lightly and butter well.

3. Place a slice of tomato, then a rasher of bacon and finally a wedge of Brie on each piece of toast.

4. Toast under the grill until the Brie melts, and serve immediately.

Bacon-topped mushrooms
Serves 4

1 tbsp vegetable oil
4 rashers bacon, chopped
2 garlic cloves, chopped
½ tsp fresh thyme leaves
30g breadcrumbs
4 large breakfast, Portobello or other large flat mushrooms
50g mozzarella, sliced into 4

1. Preheat the oven to 190°C (Gas 5). Meanwhile, heat the oil in a frying pan and fry the bacon with the garlic until crispy.

2. Remove from the heat and stir in the thyme and breadcrumbs. Trim away most of the stalk from the mushrooms. (If you wish, do so before frying the bacon and they can be chopped up and fried in the bacon mixture.)

3. Place the mushrooms on an oiled baking sheet. Top with equal quantities of the bacon mixture and then add the mozzarella slices.

4. Bake for 15–20 minutes until the mozzarella has melted and is golden.

Lentil and bacon soup
Serves 4–6

2 tbsp vegetable oil
1 rounded tsp butter
1 medium onion, finely chopped
3 carrots, diced fairly small
2 garlic cloves, chopped
150g bacon, chopped
1 tsp dried parsley
200g red lentils
1.5 litres vegetable or chicken stock
Salt and black pepper to taste

1. Heat the oil and butter in a saucepan and gently fry the onions for a few minutes.

2. Add the carrots, garlic and chopped bacon and continue to cook gently for about 5 minutes.

3. Stir in the parsley, lentils and stock, and bring to the boil. Reduce the heat and simmer for 45 minutes, stirring occasionally.

4. Allow to cool for 1 hour at least and then season to taste before gently reheating prior to serving. This allows the flavours to develop.

Tomato and bacon pasta sauce
Serves 4

Add grated Cheddar or Parmesan when serving with your favourite pasta shapes.

2 tbsp olive oil
1 small onion, finely chopped
2 garlic cloves, chopped
6 rashers bacon, chopped
2 tbsp tomato purée
350ml passata
2 tbsp freshly chopped parsley or 10 basil leaves
Salt and black pepper to taste

1. Heat the oil in a frying pan and gently fry the onion and garlic until the onion is translucent.

2. Stir in the bacon and fry for a few minutes until the bacon is cooked through.

3. Add the tomato purée and passata and season to taste.

4. Allow to simmer for 10 minutes before stirring in the herbs. Continue cooking for 5 minutes, stirring occasionally.

Cheddar, gammon and leek bake
Serves 4

2 tbsp vegetable oil
400g leeks, chopped
About 350g gammon or bacon, chopped
1 level tsp thyme leaves
700g potatoes, peeled, sliced and parboiled
150g mature Cheddar, grated
100ml double cream
50ml milk
1 tbsp fresh parsley, chopped
Salt and black pepper to taste

1. Preheat the oven to 190°C (Gas 5). Lightly butter a roasting tin or ovenproof dish.

2. Heat the oil in a frying pan and gently fry the leeks for a few minutes.

3. Add the chopped gammon or bacon and stir in the thyme. Cook gently for about 10 minutes.

4. Put a couple of spoonfuls of the leek mixture into the base of the prepared tin or dish then add a layer of potato slices and a sprinkling of cheese (reserve some for the topping). Continue layering like this and finish off with a layer of potato. Season to taste.

5. In a jug combine the cream, milk and parsley and pour over the potatoes. Sprinkle with the remaining cheese.

6. Bake for about 30 minutes until the dish is bubbling at the sides and the cheese is golden and then serve with a green vegetable such as broccoli, spring cabbage or asparagus.

Bacon and butter bean casserole
Serves 4–6

180g dried butter beans soaked in cold water overnight
2 tbsp vegetable or sunflower oil
1 medium onion, chopped
1 garlic clove, chopped
1 stick celery, finely chopped
3 medium carrots, diced
200g chopped bacon
4 tbsp tomato purée
500ml chicken stock or water
100g frozen green beans, defrosted

1. Drain and rinse the butter beans in cold water then place in a pan with sufficient hot water to cover with 4cm to spare. Bring to the boil and then simmer vigorously for 40 minutes or until tender.

2. Preheat the oven to 180°C (Gas 4). Heat the oil in a saucepan and fry the onion and garlic for 2 minutes then add the celery, carrots and bacon. Fry, stirring constantly, for 5 minutes.

3. Stir in the purée and stock or water. Bring to the boil then add the butter beans and the green beans.

4. Transfer to an ovenproof lidded dish and bake for about 45 minutes. Serve with baked or boiled potatoes.

Broccoli and bacon bake
Serves 2

200g broccoli spears
6 rashers of bacon (smoked is good in this recipe, but not necessary)
300g crème fraîche
80g mature Cheddar, grated
50g fresh breadcrumbs

1. Steam the broccoli for 5–8 minutes and grill the bacon until just crispy.

2. Place the crème fraîche in a saucepan with 50g of the cheese and heat gently, stirring. When the cheese has melted, remove from the heat.

3. Preheat the oven to 200°C (Gas 6). Place the steamed broccoli in an ovenproof dish. Chop the bacon and arrange over the broccoli.

4. Spoon the cheese mixture over the top and sprinkle with the remaining cheese and the breadcrumbs.

5. Bake for 20 minutes or until the top is brown and crispy. Serve with salad or crusty bread.

Chicken, pork and sun-dried tomato terrine
Serves 8

Vegetable oil for frying
1 small onion, finely chopped
2 garlic cloves, chopped
2 tbsp brandy
12 rashers streaky bacon, thinly sliced
400g minced pork
Pinch nutmeg
12 pimento-stuffed green olives
200g skinless chicken breasts
40g sun-dried tomatoes, drained of oil
1 tbsp chopped fresh parsley
Salt and black pepper to taste

1. Preheat the oven to 180°C (Gas 4). Meanwhile, heat the oil and fry the onion and garlic gently in a frying pan until just soft. Stir in the brandy and cook for a minute before setting aside to cool.

2. Line a 900g loaf tin with the bacon, stretching it slightly and overlapping the sides by a couple of millimetres.
Put the minced pork in a bowl and season with nutmeg and salt and pepper. Add the onion and garlic mixture and mix well with your hands.

3. Place half of the pork mixture in the tin and press down well with your hands. Arrange the olives evenly over the surface of the mince layer.

4. Thinly slice the chicken breasts and arrange on top of the olives. Press down again.

5. Slice the sun-dried tomatoes, if necessary, and place on top of the chicken and olives. Sprinkle with parsley and check the seasoning.

6. Arrange the remaining pork mixture over the tomato and

parsley layer and press down carefully. Cover the top with the bacon and place a piece of foil over the tin. Bake for 1 hour, then remove the foil and cook for a further 15–20 minutes. Cool and drain most, but not all, of the excess juice from the tin.

7. Cover with a sheet of clingfilm and put another loaf tin on top with some weights then chill overnight. Remove from the tin and serve sliced with new potatoes and salad.

Bacon-wrapped fish
Serves 2

2x 150g fillets of pollock (or any white fish such as cod or monkfish)
A little lemon juice
6 rashers of streaky bacon
Vegetable oil for greasing
Black pepper to taste

1. Preheat the oven to 180°C (Gas 4). Meanwhile, arrange the fish fillets in an ovenproof dish and season with black pepper but no salt – the bacon will be salty enough.

2. Drizzle a little lemon juice over the fish.

3. Wrap 3 rashers of bacon around each fillet and place on an oiled baking sheet. Bake for 15–20 minutes.

4. Serve with new potatoes and baked leeks, red cabbage, kale, peas, green or French beans.

Cheesy bacon bake
Serves 4

1 large onion, chopped
4 large potatoes, peeled and diced
Butter for greasing
150g Cheddar, grated (more cheese can be used if you like it very cheesy – a mixture of Cheddar and Red Leicester is good, too)
8 rashers bacon
Salt and black pepper to taste

1. Put the onion and potatoes in a saucepan, cover with warm water and season with salt. Bring to the boil and then simmer for about 15 minutes until the potatoes are tender. Meanwhile, preheat the oven to 200°C (Gas 6).

2. Drain the potatoes and onion well and arrange in a buttered ovenproof dish or roasting pan. Season with salt and black pepper.

3. Sprinkle over the grated cheese and arrange the bacon over the top in even layers. Bake for 25–30 minutes until the bacon is cooked and the cheese has browned around the edges. Serve with a green salad.

Chapter 4

Making pancetta

What is pancetta?

You might be forgiven for thinking that pancetta is basically bacon. When bought loose, sliced as lardons destined for a creamy pasta dish, it can look remarkably similar, but the product is distinct. The modes of manufacture are actually simpler than for bacon since the main ingredient is invariably pork belly, whereas bacon can be made from any cuts really, the majority being back with belly, belly and sometimes simply loin.

We make the mistake of thinking that all cured meats, particularly from southern European countries, are eaten raw. With pancetta there seems to be some confusion, because it is meant to be cooked. However, even some Italian recipes for making pancetta vary in this respect. Almost all pancetta are hung, usually for a week or ten days, but some recipes call for a two-month hanging period when the meat can be sliced thinly and eaten raw. Rightly or wrongly, I am sticking to a definition of pancetta that first of all it is cured pork belly. And that it is cured in such a way as to require cooking before consumption.

A little history

Pancetta is an ancient food ingredient dating back at least to Roman times, Legionnaires being given a sizeable piece every three days towards their ration. This simple fact belies a remarkable amount of organisation, the movement of pigs, the processing of meat, the transportation of pancetta. Since it is better to move pigs, alive and therefore fresh, and then better still to establish herds at the point of use, the Roman authorities went to great lengths to ensure butchers to kill and butcher, charcuterers to prepare pancetta and other preserved meat, and cooks to prepare the meals. While I'm not trying to claim the Romans invented charcuterie, they did introduce the pigs they liked, and many of our current breeds can be dated back to Roman occupation.

Pancetta was produced largely in Lombardy, a northern region of Milan, in the Middle Ages, where the meat was rolled before being sliced, whereas in central parts of Italy it was usually kept flat. So we have *arrotolata* (rolled and usually sliced) and *stesa* (flat and usually cut into pieces for pasta dishes, etc.).

Pancetta: how it is made and used
Pearl anniversary pancetta

The following pancetta is one that I created for my pearl wedding anniversary (that is 35 years) – hence the name. From Saxon times to the twentieth century, couples in certain counties, mainly Shropshire and Staffordshire, were awarded a flitch (side) of bacon if they could show they had not regretted their marriage for a year and a day. Even in very recent times, flitch courts still existed in these counties. I reckoned that, after all those years, the number of days that we had not regretted being married should add up to the required amount, so I awarded my wife with a 'flitch' of pancetta.

It's a simple recipe that is a really good way of starting to make your own bacon. You will need a plastic box with a lid that can be sterilised and that's about it!

>*2kg slab of pork belly, skin on*
>*75g curing salt*
>*50g soft brown sugar*
>*25g mustard powder*
>*20g crushed black pepper*

1. First of all you need to prepare the meat. This piece of belly will have ribs in it, which need to be cut out. Some recipes say to leave them in, but I prefer not to – besides, my son loves ribs! You need a good flat surface. Use a paring knife to remove the rib as close as possible, but don't cut between the bones. See also page 30, or, alternatively, you can ask your butcher to do this for you.

2. To make the cure, mix all the dry ingredients together in a bowl. Add about 10 per cent of the cure to the bottom of a lidded container.

3. With your fingertips, rub about a third of the cure over the surface of the meat except for the skin and set it skin side down in the box. Secure the lid and place it in the fridge. Leave for two days.

4. After this time, remove the meat, scrape all the cure from the surface and rinse out the box (you should find some liquor in the bottom that needs to be poured away). Repeat the process with the rest of the cure and refrigerate for another two days.

5. Remove the meat from the box and wash all the cure from the surface. Pat dry with a clean towel, wrap in muslin and store in the fridge. Leave for two days if you can (I can never quite manage it!) before testing by cooking a slice.

I find this method makes the skin very hard and difficult to cut, so I pare it away before slicing with a knife.

You will find a lot of surprises with this pancetta. Sliced and eaten like bacon, you will get mild salt, areas where the meat is sweet, still others where the meat is hot and pepper laden. If you needed convincing that homemade food is best, this will do it.

Recipes for pancetta

Pancetta Tesa

This recipe for pancetta has no sugar in it. It is an ingredient rather than a bacon you would simply eat on its own, and it is used in Spaghetti Carbonara in one of its many forms. I have also used it on pizza. Actually, if you add some chilli powder and paprika to the cure you get a product not unlike chorizo for pizza. It has to be cooked, however, unlike most chorizo sausage.

1 slab pork belly, skin removed (see page 30, or your butcher can do this for you)
Per kilo of pork you will need:
35g curing salt
2–5 garlic cloves, minced (as much or as little garlic as you like, but you must have some!)
10g crushed black peppercorns
10g crushed juniper berries (optional)

1. Remove the ribs from the pork as closely as possible with a paring knife. Transfer to a plastic lidded box.

2. In a bowl, combine all the ingredients for the cure. Sprinkle the cure all over the meat, making sure every part is covered and rubbing in with your fingertips, where necessary. Add the lid and transfer the meat to the fridge.

3. Every day for a week, turn the pork, making sure the cure is redistributed over all the surface. The meat will lose water and then start to harden. Test to see if the hardness is uniform by poking with a clean fingertip: any areas that are not hard require longer curing, so give it another couple of days.

4. Once cured, the meat needs to be washed and patted dry with a clean towel or kitchen paper towels. I use the box it was cured in for the next stage. Wash the box out and dry it completely

before returning the meat to the box, fatty side up. Return to the fridge for at least a week, preferably two. Make sure nothing can drip onto the meat or gain access to it, and avoid strong aromas in the fridge – though, to be honest, the garlic can be a little overpowering if you use a lot, and in such cases I put a clean kitchen towel on the box.

This pancetta is used in cooking, and I tend to slice it into 5mm cubes for use as lardons. If you don't have a butcher who can sell you a slab of pork belly then you can use the cut strips you get in the supermarket, remove the skin and take out the end rib.

Pancetta Arrotolata

This simply means rolled pancetta, and there are so many variations you can experiment with additional flavours. For this version the main flavours are salt, sugar and black pepper, the initial cure being salt and sugar. This version of pancetta is hung to allow it to dry, but not long enough to make it like a piece of prosciutto. It is usually sliced and cooked like bacon.

You need a piece of pork belly, skin removed and boned out. There should be a layer of fat on the outside, which is generally left intact (see also page 30, or ask your butcher to do this for you).
Per kilo of meat you need:
35g curing salt
20g brown sugar (granulated white is also fine)
30–50g crushed black peppercorns

1. In a bowl mix the salt and sugar for the cure and then rub into the surface of the meat with your fingertips. It is preferable to use a zip-lock bag to store the meat and to cure it for five days to a week in the fridge, turning frequently. The liquid drawn from the meat will continue the curing process, dissolving the external salt, and if you massage the meat through the plastic curing bag, it will cure more efficiently. Of course, you can also

cure in a dish, making sure the meat is covered with salty liquor by turning it over.

2. After about five to seven days, remove the meat, wash and pat dry as much as you can with a clean towel or kitchen paper towels. You can tell if the cure is complete: the meat will be harder, there will be a large amount of liquid drawn off and the colour will have changed to a pinkish red.

3. You can now start the rolling process. The meat is a little resistant at first, but some persistence will transform it into a roll. However, before this, on what will become your inner surface, opposite to the fat, a liberal layer of crushed black peppercorns is added. You need about 3mm of pepper – well, maybe not that exact, but a good coating, possibly about 30–50g in total. It's not about the weight, but the layer. Pat the peppercorns into the meat so they do not fall off when the whole thing is rolled and then tied.

4. The rolling of the pancetta has to be secure, with no air gaps between the surfaces. This is achieved by first of all rolling it as tightly as possible and then tying the meat along its length. The first 'loop' of butcher's twine is put in place once the meat is rolled by hand and shaped to form an even piece. At the end of the meat apply a butcher's knot (thread the twine three times around itself, and then secure with a granny knot). Make sure there is excess twine at the bottom of the meat – you will use this to tie up later.

5. Bring the butcher's twine a couple of centimetres back and make a loop round the meat with the connecting twine between the loops uppermost. The key here is to keep the tension taut. When you get to the end, turn the meat over and opposite to the top twine, run the twine around the loops, keeping it taut until you reach the bottom. Tie tightly to the tail of the twine you started off with. Finally, wrap the meat in a double layer of muslin and hang in a cool, dry, airy place for thirty days.

Recipes for pancetta dishes

Pancetta-wrapped stuffed chicken breast
Serves 4

Vegetable oil for greasing
4 large skinless chicken breasts, flattened
100g soft cream cheese (mascarpone is especially good)
2 garlic cloves, crushed and beaten into the cheese
8 slices of sun-dried tomatoes in oil
12 slices pancetta
Salt and black pepper to taste

1. Preheat the oven to 190°C (Gas 5) and meanwhile oil a baking sheet.

2. Place the chicken breasts on a work surface and spread a quarter of the cheese-garlic mixture over the surface but not quite to the edge.

3. Lay two slices of sun-dried tomato over the cheese and season with salt and black pepper, as liked.

4. Roll up the chicken as tightly as you can and secure with a cocktail stick.

5. Wrap 3 slices of pancetta tightly around each chicken breast and place on the baking sheet. Spray with a little oil.

6. Bake for 25–30 minutes. Allow to rest for 10 minutes then serve with roasted sweetcorn, new potatoes and peas.

Pancetta carbonara
Serves 2

2 large eggs
150ml double cream
100g Pecorino cheese, grated
A little olive or vegetable oil for frying
180g pancetta, cubed
200g spaghetti
Black pepper to taste

1. Beat the eggs and cream together in a jug and stir in the cheese.

2. Heat the oil in a frying pan and gently fry the pancetta until crisp.

3. While the pancetta is frying, place the spaghetti in boiling salted water and cook according to the package directions until tender (al dente).

4. Drain the spaghetti when cooked, return to the pan and quickly stir in the pancetta.

5. Quickly stir in the egg mixture, stirring well so everything is well coated. Serve immediately.

Pancetta with mushrooms and Parmesan
Serves 4–6

500g of your favourite pasta
(linguine, fusili and conchiglie are all good)
A little olive or vegetable oil for cooking
2 garlic cloves, crushed
200g pancetta, cubed as lardons
200g assorted mushrooms (button, chestnut, open cup, porcini
(soak if dried), oyster and sliced Portobello)
100g grated Parmesan cheese
250ml double cream
Truffle (optional – winter blacks are good)

1. Begin cooking your pasta in a large pan of boiling salted water according to the package directions.

2. Heat a little oil in a large saucepan and add the crushed garlic, followed by the pancetta lardons. Cook until the lardons are just browning. At this point add the mushrooms and cook for a further 3 minutes.

3. Add the well-drained pasta to the sauce and stir in the Parmesan cheese and cream. For a final flourish, you could flake some truffle on the top. Serve immediately.

Pancetta with mixed vegetables
Serves 4–6 as a side dish

400g Brussels sprouts, trimmed
2 medium-sized carrots, cut into small chunks
Vegetable oil for frying
250g pancetta, cut into small pieces
Black pepper to taste

1. Steam the Brussels sprouts and carrots together for about 5 minutes or until just tender.

2. Heat the oil in a frying pan and fry the pancetta until golden and crispy.

3. Drain the vegetables and stir into the pancetta, coating them well in the meat and juices.

4. Sprinkle with a little pepper and serve immediately.

Pancetta pasta with peas
Serves 2

2 tbsp vegetable oil
2 garlic cloves, chopped
200g pancetta, chopped
250g peas (fresh or frozen), cooked
150ml single cream
100g grated Parmesan or Grana Padano cheese plus extra to serve
200g tagliatelle or fettuccine, cooked according to the directions on the package
Black pepper to taste

1. First, heat the oil in a frying pan and fry the garlic and pancetta until golden.

2. Stir in the peas, cream and cheese and season with black pepper. Heat gently, stirring constantly, for 2–3 minutes.

3. Drain the pasta and add to the pancetta mixture. Stir to coat with the sauce and serve immediately with extra cheese and black pepper.

Chapter 5

Making prosciutto

I never wanted to produce an air-dried ham in cool, wet Lancashire but it always loomed in the background, almost accusingly – 'Am I not the pinnacle of curing?', 'Everyone else is doing it!' So it was only a matter of time before I had a go, and to be completely honest, I was never happy about it. I would worry about the ham while it was curing, while it was drying, as the mould appeared on the side, when it was sliced to be sure if it really was botulism-free, and indeed if the cut surface was now bug-free.

I had always been happier with a nice side of bacon, of boiled ham and the variations on cooked meat. But eventually, trials and concerns of incomplete curing carefully assuaged over the years, I have become more accepting and can now completely enjoy my homemade air-dried ham.

The more you read on the subject, the more you will find there are almost as many ways of making cured pork of any description – and prosciutto is no exception – as there are people making it. Some of what they do is borne out of fear of making a dangerous product. Others act blindly and with bravado, often taking unnecessary risks with the amount of salt, the temperature and technique. All I can say is these recipes have worked for me.

How to make a basic air-dried prosciutto

Below is a general outline to making a basic air-dried ham:

- Buy a ready-boned piece of pork leg, or bone one yourself (see also page 30)
- Prepare your cure – mostly just curing salt
- Apply the salt cure and press into a suitable container for around 3 to 4 days per kilo
- Wash your ham to remove all salt from the surface and dry with a clean towel or kitchen paper towels

- Weigh and wrap in two layers of muslin and hang for six months to a year in a cool dry place. It will easily last a year – the record is a hundred years!

Using salt

When dry curing a ham for air-drying it is not so much a question of how much salt to use but more to do with how long the meat is kept in the salt. It takes roughly three to four days per kilo of pork for the salt to penetrate to the centre of the meat. Consequently, you can easily work out that a ham of your weight needs such and such a length of time for curing.

These days I cure my hams in a box on which I can place a piece of wood and apply pressure from a heavy weight. It flattens the ham somewhat, but also helps force out any extra blood / liquid. For small hams I use a wooden lidded box, about 45 x 45cm and 45cm deep. I use a 20kg weight for the first week of curing.

For the cure you will need:

6–8kg curing salt
(enough to cover the whole ham by about 2cm all round)
50g mustard powder
100g cracked black pepper

To be honest, you really don't need any other flavours than salt. Nearly all air-dried hams around the world are just salted. Simply mix the ingredients together, along with any other flavours you might wish to add – juniper berries are a popular choice.

All that salt might seem expensive, but you are making a product worth well over £120 in the shops at the time of writing for a fraction of the price. Also, the leg is equally good with just salt as a cure. Later in this chapter (pages 67–72) you will find some pointers on making hams from around the world. Essentially they are no different from this recipe, but having completed this one successfully, I'm sure you can work out the rest.

Which joint to use

Traditionally prosciutto is made from the top part of the hind leg of the pig, and one that weighs about 12kg is ideal, though you can get them from 5kg upwards.

Boning and salting

It is almost certainly best to buy a boned piece of pork leg for your first attempt at air-drying. You could ask your butcher to tunnel bone your leg, but this leaves you with the difficulty of having to salt the tunnel left behind. It's best to use a boning knife and make a clean cut of it. The reason for this is to avoid any issues caused by the bone itself: pigs are different from other animals in that they usually rot from the bone outward, making the curing process slightly trickier.

1. First of all, you should locate the aitchbone (the buttock or rump bone) in the cut surface of the meat, where the joint was removed from the pig. Essentially this is the piece of hip bone housing the ball and socket joint.

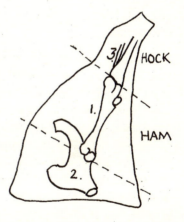

2. Carefully cut round this using a very sharp boning knife, staying as close to the bone as possible. As you do so you will find the actual ball and socket, a short way into the body of the meat from the large cut end of the joint, which you can slice through to remove the aitchbone.

1. Femur, or ham bone
2. Aitchbone (a part of the hip joint)
3. Hock bones

3. Now cut through the skin along the path of the femur (thighbone) and down to it, following the contours of the bone, cutting all round the bone to remove it. The inside can be

trimmed before being salted, reformed and the two edges sewn up with a simple blanket stitch using good strong butcher's twine and a trussing needle (both available online from butcher's suppliers).

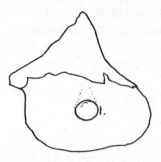

The ball joint on the end of the femur is visible on the cut surface of the ham.

1. Ball joint removed from the aitchbone

4. The end face of the meat (the piece not covered in skin) can then be completely rubbed with salt, and don't forget the other end too, where the knee would have been if it hadn't already been removed. Fill the hole with salt, ensuring no meat is left uncovered.

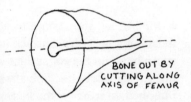

The direction of cut if you wish to bone out the ham in the curing process

5. Line the bottom of a lidded box with about 2cm cure before placing the meat on top. Completely cover the rest of the meat with salt, making sure it comes up the sides and covers the top by a couple of centimetres. Place a big board that fits the box on the top of this and then the weight, a heavy weight (I use 20kg weights). The weight is there to get as much blood as possible out of the leg.

6. Keep the ham in a cool and dry spot such as a larder or pantry (but anywhere cool and dry will do) for a week before removing the weight. There will be some liquid which makes the salt somewhat mushy. Remove this and replace with fresh cure. Re-cure the 'foot end' of the ham because seeping liquid will appear here too. Ensure the whole piece is covered with cure before replacing the lid, but this time there is no need to replace the weight.

7. Remember to cure the meat for three to four days per kilo, so a piece of 6kg pork will take roughly twenty days to cure. I know this sounds a little vague but you are looking for a real hardening of the meat and good colour change.

8. Finally, weigh your ham and keep a careful note of this for later reference.

Drying
1. Remove the ham from the cure and wash with water, patting dry with a clean towel or kitchen paper towels. Ensure the meat is as dry as you can get it.

2. Give the ham a final wipe over with ordinary malt vinegar applied with a paper towel (the smell soon disappears) and then wrap in two separate layers of muslin sheets, making sure the whole ham is covered. Tie up the top and bottom with butcher's twine. You need to tie the ham in such a way that insects cannot get into the meat and spoil it by making sure there are no gaping holes. I usually 'glue' the edges of the muslin with lard rubbed into the fabric. Special nets are available online for this purpose, but I still like to use muslin.

3. The best place to hang a ham is in a cool and airy spot that is not too windy and certainly dry. A meat safe (a cupboard or cover of wire gauze or similar material, available online) is the best place to hang, if you can keep it cool. Making hams in the winter assures this; never try this technique in the summer!

4. Hang your meat for at least six months, but preferably for ten to twelve months. When it is ready, it should smell delicious; it should also have lost about 30 per cent of its weight. At first your main indicator that your ham might be ready is the weight loss. Remember to weigh the ham in the same state as when you weighed it the first time (i.e. before you wrapped it in muslin). If there is any mould on the surface, simply cut it out and wipe with vinegar. Have a good smell of the meat – you can pierce it with a bamboo skewer and have a good smell of this too. If the

ham is off in any way it will smell bad; a sweet or clean smell is what you are looking for. It will be firm to the touch, and will last for around six months in a cool, dry place, the emphasis being on the dry!

5. Slice the meat very thinly, so a ham of any decent size will need a lot of friends to enjoy it with you! Having sliced your meat, you can seal the cut surface with lard while storing. It needs to be kept cool and, above all, dry.

Parma ham

This is Italy's favourite ham, and is a sweet cure recipe. Many people believe that air-dried hams should be more about sugar than salt, though it is still the salt that does the curing in their recipes. However, this designation of a 'sweet ham' is something of a misnomer even though we will follow the recipe with sugar here, the reason for which I will explain later.

In Parma, where the ham enjoys origin protection, Parma ham is made with only four ingredients: pig, salt, air and time. No sugar. Those who make it are trained to such a high level they are able to decide on combinations of humidity and temperature which allow the meat to absorb the minimum amount of salt. This low salt content is what makes the ham 'sweet'.

The hams are cured for about three weeks, with a change in salt halfway through, and then put to hang. They are hung for a minimum of a year in specially constructed rooms allowing sufficient movement of air. After a year they are tested using a bone needle – though it is equally possible to use wood – puncturing the meat and smelling it. And that's that, really.

It's simply not possible to replicate this manufacturing method at home, so instead we are going to use an old trick used by sausage manufacturers. Before the general use of rusk, butchers used breadcrumbs as an ingredient in sausage making. The yeast part of the bread would not be fully killed in any loaf, and in the sausage it found a nutrient-rich home. Consequently, breadcrumb sausages didn't last too long. In order to improve their shelf life, butchers added more salt. The extra saltiness was offset with the addition of sugar.

Making a Parma ham alternative

It must be said from the beginning that it is not possible to make a Parma ham without it being done in Parma! The regionality of hams, and especially Parma ham, is not just a way of protecting product names and marketing. Many people strongly believe the difference between hams is due to the microorganisms living in that particular region, in much the same way as cheese differs from one place to another. So it would be wrong to say this is a real Parma ham. Perhaps it's best to call it a 'sweet ham'. But the difference between this and the previous recipe is simple and there is no real need to go through the steps, one by one.

The difference is in the cure. For this you will need 6kg curing salt and 1kg plain white granulated sugar. Each step is the same as the basic air-dried prosciutto (pages 61) except for one, but in essence you simply use this cure. The meat is cured for a couple of days extra, about twenty-four to twenty-six days for a 6kg ham. What you get is a slightly sweeter ham that is reminiscent of Parma ham, even though the original dosen't have sugar.

A note on hams from around the world

It is not possible to actually give recipes for many of these hams for they are usually made in large- or medium-sized facilities, but their regional differences fascinate me. If you are looking for a hint as to how to make them, you can pick up some tips by studying and tasting these hams. After all, you only need to modify the basic ham recipes to get a near shot at the target.

Many, if not all, of these hams are protected under the appropriate European PGI (Protected Geographical Indication) status, so you couldn't really sell them, but there is nothing to stop you having fun in your attempts to recreate them.

Jambon d'Ardennes

Ardennes ham is made with the usual salt cure plus juniper

berries, thyme and coriander. It is smoked under oak until dark brown and then dried for at least twelve months. This is a Belgian ham, but another though very similar French Ardennes ham is produced.

The Ardennes is an area is separated by the border between France and Belgium, and is famous for its charcuterie. Here, they are so proud of their Andouille sausage, Pancetta sale sec and Jambon that they formed the Fellowship of Ham sec des Ardennes.

You can approximate this type of ham, though it won't really be Ardennes any more than homemade pâté is an Ardennes. I simply cured my boned ham of 4.5 kilos in salt for twenty-one days, then washed and patted it dry. It was then kept in a double layer of muslin for six months to dry off, and finally smoked for two days, really slowly using a mixture of oak and apple. Actually I started with oak, ran out and finished off with apple.

I say all this to point out that charcuterie is sometimes a matter of trial and error, although you should take all precautions to keep your meat safe. You must also realise that it is quite a gamble to make a ham that is going to take the best part of a year to produce, and that you may not like at the end of the day, but it's just one of the dangers of being passionate about curing!

Elenski but

This ham originates from the northern town of Elena in Bulgaria. It is simple to make, and every village in Bulgaria has its own recipe. A very fresh pork leg is salted and then placed in a barrel with a layer of bacon and salt in the bottom. The bacon is there to act as a saddle, separating the pork from the salt beneath. Salting takes place as a rub over the whole surface of the leg, the skin having been left in place. The meat is re-salted every five days for 60 days, and is then washed first in boiling water and afterwards with sauerkraut juice. It is then hung for at least a year.

You can fit a few hams in a barrel, and this ham started its existence as a community affair. The public slaughter of pigs would cause quite a stir. Normally placid people fought for burned pigs' ears in the street, and of course it was time for sausage making once the intestines had been cleaned and salted. Well, that's how it used to be. Alas, these days the state of the economy means that pigs are sold and processed more centrally and the fun of the pig harvest isn't what it used to be.

The pig is slaughtered in late autumn, allowing it to cure through the winter months, when it is cold. When hung, it is wrapped in thick muslin to keep the flies off. Sometimes it is hung for only a few weeks and it is then used for cooking. There is a fine line between pancetta and prosciutto: prosciutto is used for cooking, not completely cured or dried, while pancetta is well cured and hung and made into sliced raw ham.

Prague ham

For a while these hams were supposedly the best hams in the world. Invented in the 1850s, Prague ham is a wet cure where the brine is injected directly into the muscle. The cure was a mixture of salt, saltpetre and sugar. It is from this period that the term 'Prague powder' for saltpetre/salt mixture is coined (see also page 21). Antonín Chemel opened his ham factory in Prague in the early 1860s and the resulting hams were exported around the world, specially shaped and wrapped. It became the fundamental standard for ham simply because it was easy to slice, easy to sell and quite delicious too!

The hams were cooked and smoked then wrapped in fat and washed in aspic to give them a glaze. Later they were sold in tins and later still in vacuum-sealed packs. Early hams were boneless, but boned versions were produced later on.

You can approximate the Prague ham by wet curing a leg (allow four days per kilo) in a brine of 5 per cent of the weight of the meat and about half as much sugar (50g per kilo). If the meat is more than 10cm thick, you should inject some of the cure into the muscle.

Originally the hams were cooked in hot water, then smoked, but you can hot smoke the ham (apple is a good wood for this), either in a barbecue or in a vertical hot smoker until the surface is a uniform golden brown and the centre of the meat has reached 80°C (176°F) for at least an hour.

Once cooled, pat away the excess on the surface and vacuum pack or consume. It will freeze vacuum-packed for up to three months, but is best enjoyed fresh. You can recreate the glaze by brushing with gelatine.

Croatian Pršut

Although the process is a little long-winded, this is a very simple ham to make. It is made in two regions of Croatia: Dalmatia and Istria. There are a number of recipes for both, but it seems that the Dalmatian type has the skin left on whereas the Istrian has the skin and outer fat removed, though a search of the internet will turn up some wide variations on this. Many recipes state that the hams are simply salted with no other flavours, but then again some people add rosemary and garlic.

The main things to remember are to add 10 per cent of the weight of the salt, and the meat is salted for one day for each kilo of weight. Then the legs are washed rather well in lots of water and placed under a heavy wooden board and pressed for about a week to get any remaining blood out. Afterwards the hams are cold smoked. The differing woods seem to be a regional theme, using whatever is to hand. Smoking goes on for forty days, but I have seen examples of hams being smoked for sixty days! Finally, they are hung in caves and cellars for at least a year, but the most expensive ones are hung for two years. For me the most interesting part of this process is that nowhere is any sugar added.

Bayonne ham

When I think of ham, three wonderful cities come to mind: York, Parma and Bayonne. Bayonne is in the northern Basque region and seems remote on the Atlantic coast of France – it takes all night long to get there by train from Paris.

Bayonne ham is a simple product – sweet and not too salty, with a subtle tang. There are lots of incorrect recipes out there, some asking for salt to be added to wine to make a wet cure, which seems to be completely wrong. First of all, a huge amount of salt is placed over the ham and this is left for twelve days. The next stage involves washing the salt off the ham and covering the cut surface with a paste made from flour and lard. This is to cut down the rate at which the ham dries. Some people rub the skin with crushed Espelette peppers (a hot red chilli grown and dried in the Espelette region of the Basque Pyrenees not far from Bayonne), giving the ham a slightly piquant flavour. It is air-dried for about ten months.

Guanciale

If you simply cannot bring yourself to eat a pig's face – and I quite understand how difficult this can be, especially since they seem to smile at you from the table – you can ask your butcher to bone out the cheeks for you. Actually it is quite a difficult job because there are glands in the face that can taint the meat if they are cut open.

Guanciale is an amazing meat, which produces a product like pancetta, but deeper in flavour. The fat melts more easily, being marbled into the muscle, and gives a depth of flavour simply not available with any other cut. Guanciale is edible raw, thinly sliced, but is also found in many dishes cooked as an ingredient. Guanciale carbonara is wonderfully flavoursome as large chunks in a cassoulet. Or gently fry and serve with crusty bread dipped in the rendered fat.

Here is my take on Guanciale. You will need boned-out hog cheeks (why we call them hog cheeks just because they are the face rather than pig cheeks, I don't know!). For 2 kilos, you will need the following ingredients for the cure:

70g curing salt
5 garlic cloves, crushed and very finely chopped
60g white granulated sugar
10g crushed black pepper
4 tsp dried thyme

1. In a large bowl mix together the cure and rub it into the meat. Store in a lidded plastic container in the fridge for ten days, turning the meat daily.

2. You can test the meat to see if it is cured by pressing with your fingertips – it should be uniformly hard.

3. Remove from the cure, which should be wet because of the removal of liquid from the meat, and wash off the cure, patting dry with a clean towel or kitchen paper towels.

4. Use a skewer with some sterile butcher's twine added to make a hole in the top corner of the meat (a red-hot poker is traditionally used) and hang in a cool, dry place wrapped in muslin to protect it from insects, or in the fridge, for a month. (I use an old fridge and secure the meat to one of the wire shelves.)

Recipes for prosciutto

Prosciutto-wrapped prawns and vegetables
Serves 2–4

12 raw king prawns, shelled and deveined
A little olive oil
4 slices of prosciutto, cut into 12 strips

1. Drizzle each prawn with a little olive oil – I find the oil sprays are useful for this.

2. Wrap each prawn in a strip of prosciutto and place on an oiled baking sheet.

3. Place under a hot grill for about 40–50 seconds until the prawns have changed colour and turned opaque before serving. Or place in a preheated oven to 200°C (Gas 6) for 10–12 minutes. Serve hot.

Variations
Preheat the oven to 190°C (Gas 5). Spray asparagus tips with oil and wrap in a strip of prosciutto and oven roast for 15–20 minutes. Or wrap thin batons of carrot or courgette or strips of red pepper in prosciutto. Spray with oil and roast for 15–20 minutes. If you like your vegetables softer, steam for a few minutes beforehand. You can also slice large flat mushrooms into four and wrap with strips of prosciutto. Spray with oil and oven roast for 10–15 minutes.

Prosciutto and roasted tomato pizza
Serves 4

500g strong white bread flour plus extra for rolling out
1 tsp salt
1 sachet (7g) fast-action dried yeast
380ml warm water
1 tbsp olive oil

For the topping:
12 cherry tomatoes
1 tbsp olive oil or a spray olive oil, plus extra to grease
200ml passata
1 tbsp tomato purée
½ tsp dried oregano
1 garlic clove, chopped
150g Cheddar cheese, grated
150g mozzarella, cut into small pieces
8 slices of prosciutto
Salt to taste

1. Preheat the oven to 200°C (Gas 6). Meanwhile, make the pizza dough. Combine the flour, salt and yeast together in a mixing bowl. Pour in the water and olive oil and knead together for 10 minutes. Cover and set to one side.

2. For the topping, halve the tomatoes and place on an oiled baking sheet. Spray or drizzle with olive oil and season with a little salt.

3. Place in the centre of the oven to roast for 25–30 minutes or until golden brown and soft. Turn the oven up to 220°C (Gas 7). Oil a pizza tin and roll out the dough on a floured surface to fit the base (any leftover dough can be made into small rolls).

4. In a jug combine the passata, tomato purée, oregano and garlic and spread evenly over the pizza base.

5. Sprinkle the Cheddar over the top of the tomato base.

6. Arrange the prosciutto over the Cheddar. Scatter mozzarella on top and arrange the roasted tomatoes evenly on top of this.

7. Bake for 20–25 minutes or until the crust is a deep golden colour around the edges and the cheese is bubbling. Leave to settle for 5 minutes before slicing and serving.

Chapter 6
Wet curing and cooking ham

Is it any coincidence that the words delicious and delicate should sound so similar, or do these words have a common origin? It certainly feels like a pig's hind leg is anything but delicate, but it is delicious! Soaked in salt, perhaps with one of two other flavours, perhaps juniper berries or something sweet like molasses or honey, the ham is the sweetest and most versatile of cured meats.

The best-flavoured meat for ham

For me the flavour comes from the work done by the pig's hind legs, pushing the snout and teeth into the soil to grub up roots and herbs, and it is certainly no coincidence that the other really tasty meat on a pig is the face – all that chewing! There is one certainty in the pig world: the parts that do all the hard work end up being the most delicate, though you would hardly think of this when boiling up a head to make brawn!

It is not so easy to find really tasty pig meat these days, unlike in our grandparents' time. So much presented in supermarkets and on butchers' trays has come from the processing farm, where the animal tastes no earth, simply stands in a warm room and is given its food ration, which is as dull as the life it leads. You can easily tell such meat: study the layer of fat where it covers the muscle and you will find a crisp, clear line. Pigs that have been pampered, fed on pignuts supplemented with an excess of vegetables and nose-to-the-ground roots, maybe windfall apples and too much love, have a much less distinct line between the muscle and the fat. Some say it is a sign of overfeeding, but it's a sure sign of a happy pig! Maybe wild boar, which costs a fortune, comes somewhere close. If you can find a local pig keeper who has a couple of animals and is prepared to sell you some of the meat, you will find it's the tastiest you will ever get.

Boiled or roast ham cure

The basic boiled (or roast) ham cure is simply curing salt and sugar. There is no other flavouring because these can be added at the cooking stage. You can make boiled ham with all kinds of flavourings added – juniper berries, cloves, bay leaves, mustard, pepper and chilli. However, it is possible to make a superb ham with just salt and sugar.

I tend to make a ham, boil it until it is cooked, then add whatever flavouring I like to the surface before finishing it off in the oven for 10 minutes to glaze. Of all the recipes for wet cures, the salt content varies immensely. It is as if some of these people who publish their recipes have never actually made their ham, or in some cases have added a bit of salt just to be on the safe side, or even taken some, just to be on the safe side.

I tend to use leg for hams, small ones weighing 3–4kg, but it is possible to use shoulders, loins – any part of the animal, really. I always remove the skin, and if there is a large layer of fat then I score it, not through to the meat.

Basic boiled ham cure

400g curing salt
250g brown sugar
4 litres water

After adding the salt and sugar to the water I bring the brine to the boil, stirring until it is all dissolved, and allow it to cool before use. This removes any microbes and at the same time allows the sugar to dissolve more easily.

Looking at some of the recipes in other books, you will find huge variation in the amount of salt added to the brine. For example, one writer uses a cure using 2 kilos of salt in 6 litres of water. This is three times the amount of salt in the recipe I have given here! When writing a book like this the conundrum is 'Have I been doing it wrong all these years?' Well, the answer partly lies in the boiling of the ham, which removes a lot of salt;

you tend to lose more salt from hams to which you have added more salt, and in the end you get a very similar product. There isn't a particularly right or wrong way of making a ham, just the way that you are confident with for flavour as well as safety.

Equilibrium in the forming of cured ham

In addition to the above, the curing time leads to what is known as equilibrium. What that means is that the amount of salt in the ham and the amount of salt in the cure is basically the same. So when the ham is boiled, it loses salt to the 'pure' water. Also, the eating of the ham depends very much on the household. We, for example, demolish a ham in a few days, whereas others might take longer. If, after about five days, there is ham left, I tend to vacuum pack the final slices and freeze them – belt and braces, as it were.

You can add almost anything you like for flavour. To be honest, I can hardly tell the difference between this basic cure with or without any other flavours. Besides, the thing about ham is its succulence, moistness, salt concentration and perhaps the sweetness. Then again, even the sweetness is not that important.

Now I must be honest with you and say I rarely, if ever, smoke my ham. I just find the excess of flavour out of place in this case and much prefer the quality of the meat to shine through and speak for itself. But that's just me; in America you can hardly get a ham that isn't smoked. See Chapter 12 if you do wish to smoke your ham, though.

How much cure to use

There is an element of logic in wanting to know how much cure to use. In truth, so long as you can fit your meat into the container and cover it with cure, with plenty of room all around, it will be fine. Below is a very rough guide:

Up to 3kg of meat, use about 4.5 litres of cure
Up to 6kg of meat, use about 6 litres of cure

However, it is extremely rare indeed to wet cure large hams. Personally, I have never ever made a ham above 4kg partly because I don't have a pan big enough to cook one. And if you think about it, you would not air-dry a ham that had been wet cured – it is far too wet! You will also need the following:

Large plastic lidded container
A weight to hold the ham under the cure

The process can take different routes, partially dependent on the size of ham, but other factors are involved, as we shall see.

Dunking a ham

This is where the pork is placed in a lidded container and the cure poured on top of it. The meat has a tendency to float so you will need to weigh it down. This process takes seven to ten days, about one day for every centimetre thickness of ham. Each day the pork is turned over. The meat should be kept in a cool place. Stabbing it with a knife or skewer allows the cure to seep more easily, and does not particularly spoil the texture of the final product if done reasonably sparingly.

After a week, take a look at the meat. It will look slightly pickled and a little shrivelled. Remove the meat, wash it in water and pat dry with a clean towel or kitchen paper towels. Place on a plate and refrigerate, uncovered, for a couple of days. This gives the salt a chance to equalise through the meat. It can then be cooked.

The pump and dunk ham

This is for thicker hams, where the salt would have difficulty in getting to the centre of the meat. Brine pumps are available on the internet or from specialist cookery shops and have a wide variety of uses, from filling profiteroles to flavouring American-style BBQ joints. Using a brine pump, some of the cure is directly pumped into the meat in various places, particularly where the meat is thickest. You add 15 per cent of the weight of meat injected into the muscle. So a ham of 4 kilos would need four lots of 150ml of cure pumped into the meat in different parts of the muscle. This not only allows the salt to equalise more easily, it makes for a more uniform flavour throughout the whole product.

Once pumped, the meat is then cured in a lidded container as per the immersion method (see page 79), for a day shorter, though for large pieces of meat I usually do it for the same amount of time anyway without any problems. When ready, the meat is removed, washed, dried and left for two days in the fridge to allow the salt to pervade the meat evenly. It is then cooked. Some people say the pumped meat takes a shorter time to form consistently through the product. However, I'm in no rush, and an extra day makes very little difference.

How to cook a ham

My favourite recipe is a combination of boiling and finishing off in the oven to glaze. Roasted ham can, I think, be a little dry. There are lots of recipes out there for different styles of ham, often following country traditions, a little like sausages where still today in the UK we have Cumberland, Lincoln and so on.

You will need a large pan and something to glaze the ham. Honey, marmalade or syrup are favourites of mine, but apricot jam and maple syrup are popular too. You can also enhance the ham with cloves, pushed into the surface of the meat.

1. Place the ham in a large saucepan and cover with water. Slowly bring to the boil and then cook for 20 minutes per 500g of meat weight.

2. Remove from the saucepan and pat dry with a clean towel or kitchen paper towels. At this point you can insert cloves if you wish, or simply brush your chosen glaze over the surface. Place on a trivet in a large oven tin and bake in a preheated oven at 180°C (Gas 4) for 10 minutes per 500g of meat, or until the outer surface has become golden brown and delicious. You will

know it's right when you are tempted beyond reason to slice off the darkened surface and start eating!

3. Leave the ham to cool completely before slicing.

Roast ham

I also like to cook a roast ham slowly in a preheated oven at 150°C (Gas 2) as follows:

1. Place your ham skin side upward and with a sharp knife criss-cross cut through the skin.

2. Make a glaze by mixing 150g honey and a tablespoon of mustard. Apply this to the skin of the ham with a pastry brush to make a glaze.

3. You can poke some cloves through the skin too, if you like. I don't use too many, about four for the whole ham.

4. Cook for 35 minutes per kilo. The ham should be caramelised a little on the outside and uniformly pink and moist inside. I always use my meat probe thermometer to check that the inside is at least 75°C (167°F).

Variations on boiled ham
Cider ham

Everyone knows the link between pigs and apples, particularly in the West Country, with its tradition for orchard-fed Gloucester Old Spots. Cider ham is made with a cure of 20 per cent cider, 20 per cent apple juice and the rest is made up of water. Boil up the salt and any other flavours (cloves, peppercorns, 1 tablespoon mustard powder, sliced lemon or apple, a handful of raisins or crushed garlic) in the water first and then add the apple juice and cider. In order to make this ham you need to add the curing chemicals to a 50 per cent mixture of water and cider.

You will need:

> *400g curing salt*
> *250g brown sugar*
> *1 litre cider*
> *1 litre apple juice*
> *2 litres water*
> *Plus any flavours you prefer (see above)*

Ham shank

The lower portion of the leg, between the main muscle down to the foot, is known as the shank and is almost certainly one of the culinary joys of mankind. True, there is more connective tissue in the meat, but then again there is so much more flavour, more fat, more gelatinous and delightful eating than any other portion of the pig, except perhaps the face.

The most wonderful thing about shanks is that they are so versatile. Personally, I am happy going to Bury Market and buying a cooked shank to pick at as I wander the food hall buying fish and meat. Also, there is nothing better on a buttered muffin than cured ham shank. And it is testament to the fundamentals of this book that it is simplicity that brings out the greatest of ingredients. A ham shank butty (what we northerners call a sandwich), preferably with butter and muffin or tasty homemade bread, is just as good (avoid machine-made sliced bread, please!) as any cuisine anywhere in the world and it is all ingredient, no real flavouring. And the crowning glory of the ham shank is the meat is probably the cheapest you will find anywhere!

You will need: a large plastic lidded container and a brine made from 400g curing salt in 4 litres of water
(AND NOTHING ELSE!)

Simply immerse the shanks (skin on) in the cure and leave for three days before removing, washing them in cold water and patting dry with a clean towel or kitchen paper. I vacuum seal the cured hams and freeze, but only for cooking in various ways, such as for pea and ham hock soup (page 86). Those destined for eating on their own (a brilliant butty!) are cooked straight away.

How to cook
Simply place the shank in a pan of boiling water and cook for 90 minutes on a slow rolling simmer in a lidded pan. Check for cooking: the outer skin will look grey but the meat will be nicely pink and the fat will look wonderfully gelatinous. I always use a meat thermometer, making sure it is at least 75°C (167°F). Once checked for cooking, they are allowed to cool a little, although they are best served moderately warm – enough to make the butter on the muffin melt!

Ham shank sandwich meat
This is a simple product made from small pieces of shredded ham shank set in a stock make from gelatine. It can be made from any kind of meat, or combinations of meat, chicken and ham, which is one of our favourites.

Boil two bacon hocks for just 2 hours in the same pan. Keep an eye on the pan to make sure it does not boil dry, topping up with boiling water from the kettle as necessary. This will render the fat away, leaving the skin and meat that is very easy to pull away. Boiling the shanks in the same pan will keep the flavour in the liquor, and therefore the meat, and will result in no loss of flavour.

Keeping the remaining stock, take 250ml of it and dilute with some boiling water to make 500ml, with which you add 4 sheets of gelatine to make a jelly.

Remove the meat from the hocks to a bowl and shred with a fork. Press down as much as you can. Add the melted jelly to the meat, slowly, allowing it to permeate the meat. Place a saucer on the meat and weigh it down until it sets.

Ham recipes

Ham hock terrine
Serves 4

2 ham hocks (about 1kg each)
2 carrots, peeled if necessary, and cut into large pieces
1 onion, halved
1 stick celery, sliced
Black pepper to taste (I like to use plenty of black pepper for this recipe)
12g leaf or powdered gelatine

1. Place the hocks in a large lidded saucepan surrounded by the vegetables and sprinkle with pepper.

2. Pour over sufficient cold water to cover. Cover with the lid and bring to the boil. Reduce the heat and simmer for 2½ hours or until the meat is tender.

3. Remove the hocks from the water and set to one side to cool. Strain the stock into a jug to cool.

4. Meanwhile, line a moistened 900g loaf tin with a large piece of clingfilm and smooth out. Repeat this so you have a double layer. Leave the excess to overhang the tin.

5. Remove all the meat from the hock bones, tearing into strips and placing in a bowl.

6. If using leaf gelatine, soak in plenty of cold water for about 5 minutes, or follow the manufacturer's instructions on the package. Heat about 300ml of the cooking stock in a pan until warm and add the gelatine, stirring until dissolved. Leave to cool.

7. Lay the strips of meat in the prepared tin and pack in well to expel as much air as possible. Pour over the cooled stock to just cover the meat.

8. Seal the terrine with clingfilm. Place another similar-sized tin on top to gently weigh it down. Place in the refrigerator and leave to set, preferably overnight or 3–4 hours in a very cold fridge. When completely chilled, turn out onto a serving platter and slice. Buttered toast and a green salad goes well with the terrine. It will keep in the fridge for a week but we never have it around for that long!

Ham, leek and cheese layer
Serves 4

400g ham
1 tbsp vegetable oil
2 large leeks, chopped
Butter for greasing
2 large potatoes, thinly sliced
200g Cheddar cheese
100ml single cream
Salt and black pepper to taste

1. Preheat the oven to 190°C (Gas 5). Meanwhile, chop the ham into small pieces.

2. Heat the oil in a large frying pan and cook the leeks until softened.

3. Butter a 30cm ovenproof dish and place a thin layer of potatoes over the base.

4. Spoon a layer of leeks, a sprinkling of cheese and then a layer of ham on top. Repeat, saving a little cheese as a final topping. Season as necessary.

5. Top with the remaining potatoes, overlapping well.

6. Pour over the cream and sprinkle the remaining cheese on top. Bake for 30–40 minutes until the potatoes are tender and the top is golden brown. Serve with a green vegetable such as broccoli or cabbage.

Pea and ham hock soup
Serves 4

1 large ham hock (about 1kg)
1 tbsp vegetable oil
1 large onion, chopped
2 medium carrots, thinly sliced
½ tsp dried thyme
1 tsp dried parsley
200g dried marrowfat peas, soaked overnight in cold water
Salt and white pepper to taste

1. Place the ham hock in a large saucepan and pour over sufficient cold water to cover well. Bring to the boil and then cover and simmer for 1½ hours.

2. Remove the hock from the liquor and set to one side. Test the liquor for saltiness – this will form the stock for your soup.

3. In another large saucepan, heat the oil and cook the onion until just soft. Add the carrots and pour over the stock from the ham hock. Stir in the herbs. Season with salt and pepper as necessary.

4. Add the pre-soaked peas and bring to the boil, then simmer for 1 hour. Check to see if the peas are tender; if not, continue cooking as necessary. Top up the pan with a little boiling water if the level is dropping too much.

5. While the soup is cooking, strip the meat from the ham hock bone and cut into small chunks. Stir the meat into the soup about 45 minutes into the cooking time.

6. When the soup is cooked, keep the lid on and leave to settle for about 20 minutes before serving. The heat will be retained and the flavour is so much better than if you served it straight away. It will taste even better when cooled and reheated as necessary. When reheating, check the seasoning. However, the ham hock is salty so it is unlikely that you will need extra salt.

I like to serve this soup with fluffy dumplings. They can be dropped in about 15 minutes from the end of cooking time.

Chapter 7

Curing beef

There isn't a great tradition of curing beef products, and the reason is quite simple: economics. A prime beef animal has always been worth a lot of money and our desire for fresh beef knows no bounds. A secondary or dual-purpose animal – a milking cow, for example – often has inferior beef and therefore there is a greater likelihood that cured beef products might be developed to cope with what would be a large amount of meat, even if the animal is almost skin and bone.

It is interesting that a huge quantity of beef enters our diet processed in one form or another, in the shape of burgers, meatloaf and sausages, but very little is cured compared to pork. Another reason for this is the nature of the muscle itself. Pork generally is very fine grained, whereas beef has a more open texture, which when cured gives the meat a texture that appears to fall apart a little. This is the reason why we generally refer to cured beef as 'corned'. For years I laboured under the misapprehension that the corned beef we got in cans was actually the real thing. I thought corned beef had wheat in it – in other words, it was corned. Actually the word 'corned' refers to the appearance of the meat once salted. It forms little lumps, which in English are called corns. Wheat, maize, barley and oats are all corns – resembling little crumbs, and corned beef resembles little crumbs once salted. But the product popular on St Patrick's Day in America with boiled cabbage is a million miles away from what we get in a tin!

Some beef-cured products exist simply because of their historical context. It is said that the original biltong was created because African Boers would keep their meat beneath the saddle of the horse they were riding all day long, which was salted by the sweat of the horse and consumed by stronger men than I. Many beef-cured products have their equivalents from other meats, venison being prime, but boar, turkey and crocodile are very common in the US.

How to make corned beef

People think that corned beef is simply bought in tins or comes ready-sliced in plastic packets. Thankfully there are lots of reasons for making your own, not least because it's cheaper and it's far tastier!

Corned beef is not always served sliced but is often eaten in chunks with cabbage, or in stews. It is the basis of a number of hotpot recipes from the north of England and in the US it is frequently cooked as though it was a joint of meat.

How tinned corned beef is usually made

Corned beef is simply salt beef, like bacon is salted pork. You can 'cure' the beef in any way you like, but normally you have a cure made of salt, sugar and other flavours. Cloves are often used, as well as whatever seasonal herbs are to hand, sometimes garlic too. Perhaps the other big flavour is beer.

Butcher's corned beef is cured for a week and then it is minced and cooked, usually in sealed cans, or in the case of catering packs or for the deli, in long tins. But you can make corned beef for the family sandwiches for about a quarter the price of the bought stuff in a much simpler fashion by turning the technique on its head.

Easy corned beef

This method only takes overnight and it really works. A method I have long been using allows an exactly measured amount of salt into the product. One tip when making this is that the better quality meat you can get, the better the end product. I know that might sound obvious, but in this case it really is true. The recipe calls for minced beef, and the cheapest is very fatty, making a pretty poor product. However, if you buy brisket and mince then you will find you have a better product than if you had bought ready-minced beef. I must confess that, from time to time, during periods of financial drought, I have bought the very cheapest minced beef and found the product to be extremely fatty.

500g minced beef
7.5g curing salt
3g ground black pepper
10g sugar
50ml water (or try beer)
1 tsp mustard powder (optional)
50g breadcrumbs

1. Mix all the ingredients except the breadcrumbs together in a bowl using your hands to massage the meaty mixture. Leave for an hour and then mix together by hand again – repeat this a few times. The basic idea is that you are getting the salt through the whole of the meat, over time. You will see a definite change in colour where the meat has taken on the cure. It goes from light bright pink to a darker pink. Cover and leave in the fridge overnight.

2. The following day incorporate the breadcrumbs and mix well. The breadcrumbs are there to absorb the cooking fat and to keep the loaf of corned beef evenly textured.

3. Line a 900g loaf tin (25cm long) with baking parchment and press down the meat firmly into it. On top of this place another sheet of parchment and then another 900g loaf tin of the same length which you will fill with water to act as a press. Three-quarters fill the top tin with boiling water and place both in a preheated oven (180°C/Gas 4) for about 1½ hours.

4. Check the centre of the meat with a meat thermometer: it must reach 75°C (167°F) for at least 20 minutes. Turn out and allow to cool. The corned beef is brilliant in a sandwich, or served sliced with salad and new potatoes or in corned beef hash.

American corned beef

Generally in the UK we like our ingredients to speak for themselves, to let their flavours and freshness do the talking, as it were. However, across the pond they do like to have plenty of added flavours, and sometimes it works. Personally I prefer a very mild corned beef recipe (see page 89), but this one is flavoured with pickling spice.

You can buy pickling spice, or you can make your own. I have tried both, with not a great difference between the two, except that I like to make my own – it always adds a little something, doesn't it? Making your own is easy enough: collect the various spices you wish to add and then mix them up in a sealable jar for a few days before toasting. You can use them at harvest for pickled onions, piccalilli and other condiments. I make my own in the late summer for use when the shallots are ready for picking and I always make pickled shallots for Christmas – you simply cannot better a lump of cheese with a well-pickled shallot, but back to the job in hand …

Pickling spice ingredients
Take your pick from any combination of the following:

---

1 tbsp whole allspice berries
1 tbsp red pepper flakes
1 tbsp whole cloves
1–2 tbsp coriander seeds
1 tbsp whole black peppercorns
10 whole cardamom pods
5 large bay leaves, dried and crumbled
2 tsp ground ginger
1 tsp dill seeds
1 stick cinnamon, broken up into small pieces

Mix all the spices you wish to use in an airtight container (you need 3 tablespoons of spice to 4 litres of cure liquid) and then tip out the measured amount you are going to use in the pickle. This is placed in a dry pan and heated until you can just start to smell the aromas. I am not one for toasting spices for a long time; why fill the kitchen with the aroma when you want it in your food?

American corned beef wet cure

This corned beef recipe is a wet cure. The cure is basically sugar, salt and pickling spices in 4 litres of water for a 2kg piece of brisket. Corned beef is traditionally made from brisket, which has the right amount of marbled fat, but there is no reason why almost any cut could not be used.

The cure (for a 2kg piece of brisket)
500g Supacure curing salt
250g brown sugar
3 tbsp pickling spice
4 litres water

1. Remove the silver skin (small delicate membrane resembling fat) and surface fat and trim the meat. Place in a sealable container and cover with the cure. The meat might float and should be weighed down. A plate is usually sufficient for this, but if not, place a potato on top of the plate too. Place in the fridge and cure for seven days, turning the meat over each day. Alternatively, you could use a vacuum-sealed bag and simply massage the meat each day.

2. After curing, the meat is washed and placed in a pan. Add a carrot and a sliced onion then cover with water and bring to the boil. I have found that if you cover the meat with water by a good couple of centimetres this takes a little more salt out.

3. Keep on a rolling boil for around 3 hours, checking the temperature of the centre of the meat with a meat probe; it should be 75°C (167°F) for a good 30 minutes. Once cooked, leave to cool.

4. For slicing as corned beef, the meat is then shredded and pressed into a mould, but if you cut large pieces and serve them with boiled potatoes and cabbage you will have the archetypal American food. Keep the boiling water from the meat to cook the potatoes and cabbage – it makes them more flavoursome.

How to make pastrami

What is the difference between corned beef and pastrami? Like hot dogs and hamburgers, pastrami became popular in the late nineteenth century. It is more a food of convenience and flavour, spare time and entertainment than corned beef, which is more to do with preserving and necessity.

Many people will tell you that corned beef is brisket and that pastrami is nearer to what we in the UK call a 'skirt'. However, that's not strictly true. Both are usually made from brisket and both products are cured in the same way using salt. Corned beef is then simply boiled, whereas pastrami is boiled, often rubbed with spices and then smoked. The pastrami is sometimes hot smoked, cooked in the smoking process, and is then cooled.

Well, that's what I thought. It turns out, once you look deeply into various pastrami from around the US, that many pastramis are not smoked at all, just baked in the oven, and the smoky flavour develops *in situ* from the oven itself, splashes of fat and so on creating a slightly smoky, bitter flavour. Personally, I prefer to smoke because I don't want to mess up the oven with burning beef and I can add specific flavours rather than the somewhat sulphurous flavours from burning fat. Having added all kinds of extra flavours to the meat, it is spread with mustard and then served on rye bread.

To my mind you need a hot smoker to make your own pastrami, and there are many recipes, but I prefer the food writer and journalist Tim Hayward's recipe comprising equal quantities of black pepper and coriander seeds crushed together in a mortar and pestle. The meat is cured as per corned beef (see page 89), removed from the liquor, washed, patted dry and then covered with the pepper, rubbing it in all over.

It is hot smoked – I like apple, but stronger smokes such as oak or hickory are also good, until the internal temperature of the meat reaches 75°C (167°F). The meat is wrapped in foil and then finished off in the oven on a grill with boiling water in the bottom like a *bain-marie*. Actually I often just bake at around 180°C (Gas 4) until the centre of the meat is at 75°C (167°F) for at least 20 minutes, which can take quite a while.

An alternative is to rub the meat, once cured, with the black pepper and coriander and a couple of tablespoons of good smoked paprika, then bake in foil in the oven again at around 180°C (Gas 4) until the centre of the meat is at 75°C (167°F) for at least twenty minutes, which can take quite a while.

Make pastrami from corned beef

This recipe uses the American corned beef recipe on page 90 and turns it into a pastrami equivalent. It seems to me there are so many different pastramis in the US that it hardly matters that this is slightly different in its origin. A blogger I frequently read on the internet describes pastrami as 'corned beef with chutzpah!'

Having made your corned beef, leave it in the fridge, covered, for at least a day and then make up your rub as follows:

4 tbsp roughly ground black pepper (you want 4 tbsp of the ground rub, which is roughly 5 tbsp whole peppercorns)
1 tbsp ground coriander seeds
1 tbsp dark brown sugar
1 tsp mustard powder
1 tbsp paprika
4–6 garlic cloves, crushed and minced
2 tbsp rapeseed oil for binding

1. Combine the rub in a bowl with your hands. Cover the whole of the corned beef with the rub, rubbing in hard, and replacing anything that falls off. Place on a plate, cover and transfer to the fridge for two days.

Most of the people I spoke to about this, and it was certainly true when I made my own, say the corned beef should not be wrapped in clingfilm or foil because the rub comes away when you remove the covering. For me the temptation was too great and, sure enough, the rub came off! However, I simply replaced it as I unwrapped it, pressing it home as best I could.

Smoking

I used the barbecue because I had no option, but you can smoke/cook the meat in a hot smoker, setting it to 100°C (212°F) (I used apple wood). All I did was to set the bell barbecue going with a small quantity of charcoal and then added small amounts of wood at a time. I wanted a delicate smoking, nothing too heavy – there are enough flavours going on as it is! I smoked the meat for 2 hours and then popped it in a preheated oven (160°C/Gas 3) until the centre of the meat reached 75°C (167°F) for at least 20 minutes.

Once the pastrami has cooked, leave to cool and then refrigerate for at least a day before serving.

How to make pressed beef

This is a great dish that was once so popular in the UK it was served in almost every household, but is now hardly ever seen. It starts with the curing of a piece of brisket just as though it was corned beef, and then the resulting meat is cooked and pressed overnight. Finally it is sealed with a jelly made from the cooking liquid.

2kg brisket
2 large carrots, sliced
2 large onions, quartered
1 stick of celery
3 pig's trotters

First, the brisket is cured for seven days (see page 92) in a cure made up as follows:

580g Supacure curing salt
200g brown sugar
3 tbsp pickling spices (see page 91)
4 litres water

1. Following the curing process, the beef is cooked with the carrots, onions and celery, covered in water for a good 2 hours. Use a meat thermometer to check that the meat has been 75°C (167°F) for at least 30 minutes.

2. Remove the meat from the stock, transfer to a plate and place another plate on top. Add a heavy weight on top of this to press overnight. Strain the stock into a saucepan, add the pig's trotters and boil for 2 hours, making sure the liquid doesn't boil away and is eventually reduced by a half. Remove any scum and then remove the trotters and allow to cool. Beneath the fat you should have a good jelly.

3. Transfer the meat to a serving dish and pour melted jelly over the top. Leave to set in the fridge or somewhere cool, such as a pantry. Personally, I think it's best that the jelly is not cooled too quickly so I leave mine covered and out of the fridge. It will take a few hours to set.

How to make biltong and jerky

The thing about these air-dried meats is that they can be made reasonably quickly more or less from any meat. They can also incorporate any flavours you choose. Having said that, traditional beef is the most popular choice and consequently features in the recipes in this chapter. But you can also make biltong and jerky from turkey, pork, wild boar or venison – pretty much any meat.

The difference between the two, biltong being from South Africa, jerky from the Americas, seems to be in the way the meat is cut prior to curing and drying. Biltong is thicker and some jerky is actually made from a paste and dried. However, if you search the internet you will read all kinds of claims about the superior qualities of one over another.

Biltong was made from whatever game was shot at the time, so it could be beef but equally it might be goat, gazelle, gnu or ostrich. In these modern times it is more usual to use beef. In America, the story is much the same. Jerky, the biltong equivalent, could be made from beef, buffalo, possum or even alligator.

This recipe is very simple and essentially almost not cured – though it is! (You'll soon get the idea.) Simple ingredients that are widely available are used and the meat is then cooked very, very slowly at the lowest setting of your oven. It is best if you use a convection (fan) oven, and if your oven has a defrost setting, so much the better. Whether this is biltong or jerky, I really don't know!

1kg brisket
500ml Worcestershire sauce
250ml soy sauce
200ml apple cider vinegar
1 tsp cayenne pepper
1 tbsp red pepper flakes
5g sea salt
1 medium onion, very finely chopped
4 garlic cloves, crushed and grated

1. First, thinly slice the steak – you want it to be about 5mm thick, 3cm wide and roughly 10cm long.

2. Mix all the ingredients for the marinade together in a dish and infuse the onion and garlic in the marinade.

3. Place the slices of steak in the marinade, cover and leave overnight or for at least 12 hours in the fridge.

4. Remove the meat from the marinade and wipe dry, removing any onion from the surface.

5. Set your oven to its lowest temperature. If it goes as low as 40°C (104°F) or lower, then you need to cook the meat on a rack for about 12 hours. However, many ovens have a minimum of about 75°C (167°F), where you will need about 7 hours. Turn the meat every couple of hours.

6. Test the meat for readiness – it should be dry and not squidgy. If you are in any way unsure about it, give it another hour and retest.

Vary this recipe by adding a tablespoon of honey to the marinade and 100ml boiling water to help dissolve it. You can also smoke your biltong, either by using one of the artificial methods, liquid or powdered smoke, or in your cold smoker (see

Chapter 12, for smoking instructions). Personally, I prefer to hot smoke.

Biltong
This is made from good-quality steak. I tend to use sirloin and made a kilo at a time, until my son Joshua came home from university (he's a weightlifter) and so now I make 2 kilos. It is pricey, but you get a great product.

Start by trimming most of the fat from the meat. Don't try to get the marbling out! Actually, many people prefer venison for biltong because it is a lot leaner. You need a lidded plastic box for this recipe.

Having trimmed the meat, it needs to be cut into lengths of around 20cm and by no more than 1cm thick. The curing ingredients are as follows:

Sea salt
Worcestershire sauce
Coriander seeds
Cracked peppercorns

Note: I haven't given any quantities, you are simply adding and layering at this stage.

1. Lightly sprinkle the meat with a thin layer of salt – enough to touch the meat but not so much as to cover the base.

2. Add your first layer of meat and splash with sufficient Worcestershire sauce to coat it. Then sprinkle sea salt sparingly over the meat – this isn't a coating, just a heavy seasoning.

3. Add a sprinkling of coriander seeds, then peppercorns – go particularly sparingly with the pepper. Once this layer is done, repeat with the layers of meat. Close the lid of the box and leave in the fridge for seven days.

4. At the end of this period, remove the meat and wash and pat dry with a towel or kitchen paper towels. Now start the dehydration process as follows.

I use a dehumidifier on its lowest setting, and it takes about three days to dry the meat completely. It will change colour from dark brown to a really dark brown. Your nose is the best arbiter of the meat's fitness to eat – it should smell sweet, almost neutral. Certainly 'off' smells are a sign that the meat needs to be thrown away. Also, the meat should not be spongy, but fairly hard to the touch.

If you don't have a dehumidifier you can use a box with gauze in the sides so it can be hung, the biltong completely protected on all sides from insects. Drying cabinets with temperature and humidity controls are also available. It is humidity that is the enemy of biltong, so the drier you can make it, the better. It can take ten or even twenty days in a box to completely dry biltong. Kept in a dry container, the biltong should last a couple of weeks but in our house it rarely does!

In America they have a process where they use minced (or ground, as they call it) meat and add to it various seasonings bought in packets from the supermarket. Usually these are barbecue-type seasonings known as 'rub' in the States. Sometimes they add salt to them, often they don't. Following this, the meat is seasoned and then stuffed into a jerky gun, which resembles a large ratchet-action mastic gun – the kind of thing you seal windows and bathrooms with. The resulting material is usually smoked and cooked – or hot smoked. The only real advantage with this process as far as I can see is that it allows you to use up off-cuts and various pieces of meat, and cheaper cuts, but in terms of curing for keeping, there is one problem. Once minced, the meat has an amazingly large surface area, making it more susceptible to infection. Consequently, it needs more salt, and in my opinion too much more salt to make it safe over time.

How to make bresaola

This is air-dried beef, which has been salted and spiced, but generally it is the flavour of the beef that is needed here, rather than biltong, etc., where different flavours come to the fore. It comes from Lombardy, northern Italy, and only meat coming from this region is permitted to be called bresaola. However, there are versions from all around the world generally known as beef prosciutto.

There are lots of bresaola recipes out there, some calling for more salt than others, some calling for exact temperature and humidity controlled drying, still others saying you can easily make it in the kitchen. One of the problems is the humidity – if it is too low then the meat dries out too quickly, giving a hard outside through which water cannot escape from the inside of the meat. This means the meat could easily be unsuitable for consumption although the outside 'skin' might seem to be fine.

Personally I combat this with a number of techniques. I check the meat every day or so with the nose – bad smells are a giveaway. Every few days I feel the meat through the muslin to see how it is hardening up, and every week or so I check the surface for mould. White mould is no trouble at all. Grey mould I do worry about, but I remove it with a paper towel dipped in vinegar. Any other colours I am not at all happy about and so I tend to discard the meat. But as I have already said, the nose is the first arbiter of the quality of the meat.

You don't need much of this product to go a long way, so you are not forever making bresaola in the same way as bacon. We tend to make it for special occasions and to use it in salads, no ordinary salads either. Try quartered figs wrapped in bresaola, lightly grilled! Traditionally it is served with a drizzle of olive oil and lemon juice, or flaked Parmesan cheese and rocket salad.

Make up a cure as follows, per kilo of meat:

45g curing salt
3 tsp sugar
2 tsp crushed peppercorns

Have about two teaspoons of fresh rosemary leaves ready for adding to the cure later. You can add small amounts of any flavours such as juniper berries, thyme or cloves. Keep to about 3g of these per kilo of meat.

1. A piece of silverside (known as Eye of Round in the US) is good meat to use and you need 1–2kg in weight. Any good single piece of muscle is fine. Make sure it is as fresh as can be, not frozen. Trim it well, removing all the fat from the outside and any silverskin (which is basically the connective tissue).

2. Place the meat on a large platter and very thoroughly rub the cure mixture into it. This is the most important step in the whole process. Then either put your meat in a vacuum-sealed bag or a ziplock, or a glass lidded container. Add the remaining cure, including what is left on the plate that didn't adhere to the meat. Then add the rosemary too, as whole leaves. At this point you can also add any other flavourings of your choice in small amounts (see above).

3. Cure your meat in the fridge for about twenty days. I would say a minimum of two days per 100g of meat, turning daily and massaging the meat in the liquid that has been produced by the curing process. Once cured, remove and wash the meat, patting dry with clean kitchen paper. Now get your nose in close and take a sniff of it. At this stage there should be nothing but sweetness about it, and the meat will have shrunk and will be somewhat harder.

4. Weigh your meat, keeping a careful note of this, and wrap in previously sterilised dry muslin (boil and let it dry before use). Wrap in one layer, tying at the top and bottom with butcher's twine, and add another layer in exactly the same way. It will now need to be hung for some weeks to slowly dry out. Many people use exact systems to maintain humidity and temperature control. What we often miss is that much of Italy is mountainous, giving the climate a marked UK feeling. Here you will see bresaola in meat safes drying naturally outside the house, sometimes in sheds and sometimes in cellars. So long as you keep a close eye on your cured meat, a cool place with not much wind, just enough breeze to gently change the humid air and certainly no moisture, will be fine.

5. After a week, check your meat. It should be pliable, not too heavily browned. More than anything you are looking for evidence of spoiling microbes, which means a bad smell. Blooms on the meat are fine so long as they are white, perhaps blue, but certainly not red or black. Use a vinegar-soaked paper towel to remove them. Wrap in fresh muslin and test in a couple of weeks. You will find it is a real effort, at least I do, not to slice into it at this stage!

6. Weigh your meat every week and hang until you get a 30 per cent reduction. Remove and refrigerate. Slice thinly to serve.

How to make ox tongue

I never got on with tongue, and everyone in my family looked at me with disgust. For me it was something about the flavour, not the fact that it was a tongue. It was a little like corned beef but with a metallic flavour.

Actually, all I remember from my childhood is tongue sandwiches. It was a staple of northern England because it was cheap, along with luncheon meat, black pudding, bacon, sausages, brined ribs, ham hock and pea soup. On the whole, those ingredients formed a large part of the everyday diet. It wasn't until I tasted my own ox tongue sandwiches that I began to enjoy them. Sliced more thickly than the thin slivers of metallic, strangely grained meat on a 'butty' and served with a caper sauce, this meat is superb!

Ox tongue is, perhaps, the ugliest piece of meat you will have to deal with and certainly looks rather alien-like when you are preparing it. First, it is salt brined for a week and then there is the somewhat grisly process of peeling the skin off. This transforms the meat into something deliciously edible.

1 medium onion, quartered
3 carrots, chopped
A few bay leaves
4 garlic cloves, peeled
A handful of parsley

Cure

2 litres water
1 tsp cloves
1 tbsp peppercorns
4–5 bay leaves
4 garlic cloves, crushed
500g sugar (I prefer brown, but any sweetness will do)
750g Supacure-type curing salt
1 ox tongue, about 1.5kg

1. Place all the ingredients apart from the tongue in a large saucepan and bring to the boil. Simmer for about 15 minutes until the salt and sugar have dissolved and the liquid is clear. Leave to cool completely.

2. Pour the mixture into a plastic lidded container and add the tongue, making sure the whole of the meat is covered. (I have done this twice – the first time the meat sank completely, and the second time it floated and needed to be weighed down with a small plate.) Cure for a week in the refrigerator, turning the tongue over every other day or so.

3. After a week the tongue will be much harder and darker in colour. Remove from the cure and wash under the tap to remove any excess cure from the surface.

4. Place the tongue in a large saucepan and cover with water (about 4 cm above the tongue). Add the onion, carrots, bay leaves, garlic cloves and parsley. Bring to the boil, cover the pan and reduce the heat to a slow simmer for 1 hour 30 minutes, occasionally removing any scum that forms on the top of the liquid.

5. Test the centre of the meat – it should be at least 75°C (167°F) – and then give it a further 10 minutes.

6. Remove the meat from the pan and leave to cool a little to make it easier to handle (it will firm up). Use a sharp boning knife to remove the skin and shape the meat into an appetising shape.

7. If liked, you can reduce the poaching liquor to about 20 per cent of the original (roughly 3 hours but up to 5 hours,; the amount of time varies) and press the meat. This needs a dish press, but you can make do with just an ordinary dish. The idea is that you slice the tongue along its length and then pack into a dish, pouring the liquor over. Allow to set and then refrigerate.

Recipes for cured beef products

Corned beef layer
Serves 4

2 tbsp sunflower or vegetable oil
1 onion, finely chopped
1 leek, finely chopped
2 medium carrots, diced
300g corned beef, cubed
3 tbsp tomato purée mixed with 4 tbsp water or beef stock
A dash of Worcestershire sauce
Butter to grease and for topping
4 medium-sized potatoes, sliced and simmered for 5 minutes in boiling salted water
Salt and black pepper to taste

1. Preheat the oven to 190°C (Gas 5). Meanwhile, heat the oil in a large frying pan and cook all the vegetables together until softened. Add the corned beef and cook for 2–3 minutes.

2. Stir in the tomato purée and stock mixture and add the Worcestershire sauce. Season with pepper and check for salt as the corned beef is already quite salty.

3. Butter a 30cm ovenproof dish and arrange a layer of potatoes over the base, overlapping to retain the moisture of the dish. Spoon a layer of the corned beef mixture over the potatoes and then add another layer of potatoes in the same way.

4. Repeat until all the ingredients are used up, finishing with dots of butter over the last layer of potatoes. Bake for 35–40 minutes until the potatoes are darkened at the edges and cooked through. Serve with salad.

Corned beef stuffed tomatoes
Serves 4

Butter to grease and for topping
250g corned beef, shredded
200g Cheddar, Edam, Gouda or Red Leicester cheese
1 medium egg, beaten
100g wholemeal breadcrumbs
2 tbsp tomato purée
4 large beef tomatoes
Olive oil for drizzling
Black pepper to taste

1. Preheat the oven to 190°C (Gas 5). Meanwhile, butter an ovenproof dish.

2. Put the corned beef, cheese, egg, breadcrumbs and tomato purée in a bowl. Season with pepper and mix well together with your hands.

3. Slice the tops from the tomatoes and carefully scoop out the insides with a spoon. Combine with the corned beef mixture.

4. Arrange the tomato shells in the prepared dish and fill with the corned beef mixture. Dot each one with butter and replace the lids. Drizzle a little olive oil over the top and cover the dish with foil.

5. Bake for 30–40 minutes, removing the foil after 20 minutes. The potatoes will be darkened, with cracked skin. Serve with baked potatoes and a salad.

Classic pastrami on rye
Serves 1

2 slices of rye bread
Butter
3 slices of pastrami
1 tomato, sliced
1 pickled gherkin, thinly sliced
1 tsp mayonnaise
½ tsp English mustard

1. Butter one slice of bread and place it on a plate. Layer the pastrami, tomato and gherkin slices on top.

2. Combine the mayonnaise and mustard in a bowl and spread over the other slice of bread. Top the filling with the slice of bread and enjoy immediately!

Quick pastrami and tomato sauce
Serves 4

1 x 500ml carton of passata
150g chopped pastrami
Salt and black pepper to taste
Grated Parmesan cheese, to serve

1. Simply bring the passata to a simmer in a saucepan and stir in the pastrami. Season to taste with a little salt and pepper and pour over your favourite cooked pasta shapes (farfalle works well here). Top with grated Parmesan.

Bresaola shooter sandwich
Serves 4–6

1 large round loaf of fresh bread
1 tbsp vegetable oil and a knob of butter
6 large flat mushrooms, very finely chopped (by hand or in a food processor)
1 garlic clove, chopped
4 tbsp olive oil
300g bresaola, sliced
2 beef tomatoes, thinly sliced
1 little gem lettuce, leaves torn apart
English mustard to taste
3 tbsp white wine vinegar
Salt and black pepper to taste

1. Slice the top off the loaf a few centimetres deep and scoop out the centre of the loaf. You can use this to make soft breadcrumbs and freeze for later use.

2. Heat the vegetable oil and butter together in a frying pan and fry the mushrooms and garlic.

3. Drizzle 1 tablespoon olive oil over the surface of the loaf. Spread the garlicky mushroom mixture over the base and up the sides of the loaf.

4. Add layers of bresaola, beef tomatoes and lettuce until everything is used up. Season to taste.

5. Mix the remaining olive oil, mustard and wine vinegar together and drizzle over the filling (it can also be drizzled over the top of the loaf too). Place the lid back on top and wrap in greaseproof paper and foil.

6. Place the loaf on a baking sheet and put an upturned plate on top. Transfer to the fridge. Weigh down – cans of baked beans are good for this. Balancing everything can be a bit tricky so take care! Refrigerate overnight.

7. Slice the loaf into thick portions and serve cold. However, you can also reheat it, still wrapped in the foil, if you prefer it hot.

Chapter 8
Potted meats, pâtés and confits

Using fat to preserve meat and offal

Just married, it seemed my whole life glistened with new culinary experiences. In the early 1980s there seemed to be a lot of really wholesome restaurants in Manchester. The Danish Food Centre, now sadly defunct, served up the most amazing selection of wonderful fish, caviar, gravlax, pickled herring and soused hog's face. Next door to this was an Italian place, now long gone too, serving up simple burnt-at-the-edges pizza that tasted wonderful – tomato with garlic and oregano, cheese and an extra, often asparagus, or the freshest of peas or beans. I once had lettuce hearts as a topping – quite possibly the finest pizza anywhere. Now they come with names like 'Meat Feast' or 'Volcano'.

The one food that always evaded me was pâté and I first experienced it in these two adjacent restaurants. Homemade pâté covered in butter and served with warm buttery toast. Later, at a pub called the Lancashire Fold, I was treated to my first Tornedos Rossini (steak topped with pâté) and it was out of this world!

Pâté was, to me at least, an ingredient, and it took me a while to realise it was a preserving method, largely for offal. The whole idea is that the pâté is cooked and then sealed with butter while still piping hot. (I used to get into trouble when I was younger, innocently believing the butter on the top of the pâté was to spread on my toast before applying the pâté itself! Then again I still find myself in trouble for preferring my steak well done rather than still mooing.) The principle is a simple but effective one. Fat is not only impervious, it does not provide a good environment for microbes either. So very hot food, covered in fat (in this case melted butter), should have a preserving element to it. Pâté will last about ten days refrigerated. Actually it will last even longer, but it's best not to push these things.

The eagle-eyed among you will recognise the similarity

between pâté and confit, which is essentially meat that is cooked in fat and then allowed to cool so that the fat solidifies around the meat, making the same kind of seal as the butter in a pâté. There is no real need for salt in either of these methods, save that for good seasoning, the only preservation is afforded by the heat of cooking, the seal, and maybe the odd drop of brandy or other spirits added to the recipe.

You can, of course, mix both offal and other meats to make all kinds of pâtés, though offal is really cheap and it's a good idea to get the freshest ingredients available. This might mean a visit to your local butcher, though your supermarket – and it pains me to say this – can often be fresher. There are many butchers who get weekly deliveries of offal along with their meat, and quite frankly, if it comes on Wednesday and you try to buy some on the Tuesday then you may well find your chicken livers are a little substandard, no matter how much the butcher smiles at you when dishing them up.

Whenever I buy meat at the supermarket I always go to the actual meat counter, avoiding the shelves, and I never make pâté with offal that has been frozen. The keeping property of homemade pâté is a moot point. If the seal of butter remains unbroken then it should keep in the fridge for up to ten days. However, once the seal is compromised it will deteriorate rapidly and should be eaten within a couple of days. This is because the surface area of the pâté is quite large and there are lots of opportunities for cross-infection from the atmosphere and the rest of the kitchen.

Pâté recipes

Chicken liver pâté
Serves 4

200g butter
½ onion, chopped
200g chicken livers, sliced
2 garlic cloves, chopped
Pinch thyme
½ tsp mustard powder
1–2 tbsp brandy
30g freshly made breadcrumbs
1 tbsp double cream
Salt and black pepper to taste

1. In a frying pan melt about 30g of the butter and gently fry the onion until softened. Add the chicken livers and fry over a low heat until lightly cooked, about 3–4 minutes.

2. Add the garlic, thyme, mustard powder and the brandy, stirring well. Season to taste, remove from the heat and leave to cool. Transfer the mixture to a food processor and add the breadcrumbs.

3. Melt 120g of the remaining butter. Whizz together the mixture in the food processor until smooth, adding the butter and cream as it blends. When smooth, spoon into individual dishes or one small rectangular dish.

4. Melt the remaining butter and pour over the pâté to seal. Leave to cool and then chill for 2 hours before serving. The pâté will keep for up to ten days in the fridge, unopened, and up to five days once opened.

Pork pâté
Serves 6–8

300g pork liver
300g pork shoulder, leave some of the fat on
300g streaky bacon
2 garlic cloves
1 tsp salt
½–1 tsp black pepper
1 level tsp thyme leaves or ½ tsp dried
¼ tsp grated nutmeg
30ml brandy
10 black peppercorns
3 bay leaves
Butter for greasing

1. Mince the pork liver, pork shoulder and bacon together in a food processor until the mixture resembles coarse breadcrumbs.

2. Add all the other ingredients except the bay leaves and black peppercorns. Whizz together for a few seconds. Cover and leave in a cool place for 2 hours to allow the flavours to develop.

3. Preheat the oven to 150°C (Gas 2). Meanwhile, grease and line a 900g loaf tin with baking parchment. Press the pork mixture down into the tin very firmly.

4. Press the black peppercorns evenly into the top of the pâté and arrange the bay leaves down the centre. Cover the top with foil.

5. Place the tin in a roasting pan and fill the pan with hot water to halfway up the tin. Bake in the oven for one hour and then remove the foil and cook for a further 20–30 more minutes. Cool completely.

6. Place a piece of greaseproof paper over the top of the pâté and transfer to the fridge. Weigh the top down with either weights or food cans (around 400g will do). Leave like this overnight before slicing.

Confit

This is very popular in the Basque region of France and Spain, but was once universally used. The whole idea is to keep cooked meat covered in an impervious layer of fat. Often the fat is rendered from the animal itself, but this is not completely necessary. In a way, refrigeration has sounded the death knell for confit, except it is really tasty and very easy to do. It is also the starting point for a great pâté-like dish known as rillettes, a meat paste to be eaten on toast.

What is really interesting is that the meat isn't particularly greasy – you get a product that is kind of equivalent to pulled pork. The meat is salted for at least a day, better for two days, and then cooked at a lower temperature than you would normally. On the whole it is cooked at around 95°C (203°F) for four hours. The meat is cooled with the fat covering it, and once it has set it will keep, covered, in the fridge. It is said that the meat will keep for months, but this isn't a priority for me, and I would really worry about a product that was kept for such a long time with what is, after all, only a short salting time. For this reason I would suggest that a confit like this is kept for a maximum of two weeks.

Perhaps the real reason for making confit is the flavours and textures that can be achieved. For example, re-cooked confit duck or chicken, baked in the oven, has wonderfully crispy skin.

When you come to use the confit, simply warm the container until the fat melts, remove the meat and wipe off the excess fat. It can be served as is, re-cooked or pulled to make any number of dishes.

The fat of choice is duck, though traditionally it is rendered from the animal itself by slowly cooking the fat under the skin. (Actually you can add the skin too – it makes great crackling!) Remove the skin and fat and cut into small pieces, placing in a pan – an open, flat frying pan is best. Cook slowly over a moderate heat, spooning off the fat as it melts. Leave to cool and then refrigerate.

Confit duck
Serves 2

This recipe is for 4 duck legs with thighs attached. It contains quite a few flavourings, which you can modify or remove as liked.

4 tbsp curing salt
4 garlic cloves, crushed and chopped
2 tsp crushed black pepper
1 tsp English mustard powder
Enough duck fat to cover, which is about 800g, but if you have too much then it can be allowed to cool and used elsewhere

1. For the cure, put all the ingredients except the fat in a plastic container and mix well. Make a layer from 1 tablespoon of the mix in the bottom of a plastic lidded container. Pack the duck into this and completely cover with the rest of the salt mix cure. Ensure the duck is completely coated in cure. Put the lid on and leave in the fridge for two days.

2. Preheat the oven to 150°C (Gas 2). Meanwhile, remove the duck from the container, rinse off the excess salt cure and pat dry with kitchen paper towels.

3. Place the duck legs in a bakeproof dish and melt the fat in a saucepan. Pour the fat over the duck, making sure all the pieces are covered with fat with no overlap and the meat is completely covered on the top.

4. Cook for around 4 hours. Start with the oven set at 150°C (Gas 2) and see how the fat responds. The occasional bubble is perfect but very regular bubbles are far too many, so adjust the oven temperature accordingly.

5. Once cooked, the dish is simply allowed to cool, solidifying the fat around the meat. Cover and refrigerate overnight once cold. The legs are removed from the fat as required and used in a number of ways. First, scrape as much of the fat away as

possible. Serve simply with salad, or sauté with a few shallots, garlic and 100ml freshly squeezed oranges then serve with roasted new potatoes.

Rillettes

Duck rillettes
Serves 2

This recipe uses the Confit Duck recipe on page 115. In processing this meat you are likely to introduce microbes from handling and processing, so be sure everything is kept as sterile as possible. There is a choice when it comes to the use of the skin: you can remove and bake it so it is crispy, and then break it up to sprinkle the crispy skin on the top of the rillettes, or simply incorporate the skin into the rest of the meat. The baked skin is called rillons.

Remove the meat from the confit dish and shred into a food processor then pulse until it is more finely shredded. Some people like it as a paste, others less so. Check for seasoning – it should be salty already but you might like extra pepper. Spoon into ramekins and then place in a *bain-marie* in a preheated oven at 180°C (Gas 4) for 20 minutes.

While the rillettes are cooking, melt some butter or some of the confit fat. Once the meat has cooled, pour over to seal. Rillettes is traditionally served with a bay leaf pressed into the solidifying butter.

Wrapped in foil, it will keep a week in the fridge, although traditionally it was kept in the larder. Like pâté, it is frequently served with warm toast and is also ideal with baguettes for a picnic.

Pork rillettes
Serves 4

Rillettes is frequently made with pork belly because it is first of all a very flavoursome meat and also very fatty.

From 1.5kg of pork belly, remove the bones and gristle and also the skin (see page 30, or your butcher can do this for you). The skin is then scored and baked to form rillons as described on page 116. The pork is roughly sliced and seasoned then cooked slowly in water for about 4 hours, along with 4 crushed garlic cloves, a couple of sprigs of rosemary and black pepper.

Keep the water topped up as it boils away, but maintain a very slow heat – around 90°C (194°F). After the cooking time, drain the liquid into a pan and allow it to cool. Once it is really cold it will have rendered fat that you can remove and use as a seal.

Place the meat in a food processor and pulse roughly, or chop it up with a knife into small pieces if you prefer. Check for seasoning and pack into ramekins. The pork fat, having been decanted into a bowl, can now be melted as necessary and poured over the top of each ramekin. Alternatively, use melted butter instead. Once cool, it will keep, covered, for one to two weeks in the fridge. Serve with toast and a green salad.

Potted meat

Potted beef
Serves 12

Potted beef is an ancient way of preserving beef. I remember those tiny sandwich paste pots you used to get at school Christmas parties on half-finger buns. To me they seem somewhat metallic in taste, sort of OK, but who cares when you're a five-year-old filling your face with as much as you can? However, real potted beef is another thing altogether. Is it a pâté or is it a confit? I'm not really sure. Certainly it uses butter as a way of preserving, essentially cooking the meat and then sealing it with melted butter, keeping out all kinds of microbes. Also, butter incorporated in the meat improves its keeping qualities.

Lots of recipes call for anchovies, pushed into a beef joint using a larding needle (available online). Others call for oysters, possibly to make the meat go further. This combination of fish and beef is very ancient, and is also seen in many old pie recipes from Tudor times and beyond. The fish gives the meat a richness and, more importantly, makes it cheaper! Potted beef is not salted per se except for flavour.

1kg beef (any lean beef is fine – remove any surface fat and silverskin from the joint)
2 tsp black pepper
½ tsp mace
¼ tsp nutmeg
1 tsp lovage, chopped
4 bay leaves
4 garlic cloves, halved
250g butter, cubed, plus another 250g to cover the meat at the end
Salt to taste

1. Preheat the oven to 150°C (Gas 2). Meanwhile, put the meat into a casserole and cover with the remaining ingredients, finally placing the cubed butter over the meat.

2. Cook in a slow oven – often 4 hours is not too long. You could also complete this step very easily in a slow cooker. Check it regularly – you are looking for the meat to simply fall apart.

3. When cooked, remove the meat and let it cool. Once cool, pull the meat to pieces, placing it in a clean glass bowl. The cooking juices will have a layer of butter on the top – you want to incorporate this solidified butter into the meat too, and then everything is either chopped into a uniform mass, placed in a blender (which can be a little harsh), or, the best plan, put through a mincer. You can salt to taste at this stage.

4. Preheat the oven to 180°C (Gas 4). Meanwhile, sterilise some ramekins by rinsing with boiling water and patting dry with kitchen paper towels. Fill to within 1cm with the meat mixture. Put the ramekins in a *bain-marie* of boiling water and place in the oven for 30 minutes.

5. Leave the ramekins covered while the meat cools so you can handle each ramekin. Meanwhile, melt the remaining butter and at this stage pour 1cm melted butter over the meat in each ramekin to seal. Allow to cool completely before transferring to the fridge, covered in clingfilm, where they will keep for a week.

Potted chicken
Serves 8

This is a simple recipe for potted chicken, which can be adapted to taste. Here, I have only used basic ingredients, but you can hot it up with chillis, garlic or paprika – anything really.

*6 boneless chicken thighs (skin-on for a better flavour,
but remove if preferred)
1 medium onion, quartered
1 carrot, roughly chopped
500ml water
1 tsp black peppercorns
½ tsp mace
300g butter
Salt and black pepper to taste*

1. Boil the chicken thighs along with the onion and carrot in the water for about 40 minutes on a rolling simmer. When cooked through and coming off the bone, remove the meat and reduce the cooking stock until it is about 3–4 tablespoons.

2. Transfer the chicken to a food processor, adding the liquid, black peppercorns, mace and half the butter. Blitz until you have a fine paste then season to taste.

3. Transfer to a ceramic dish and flatten the top of the paste with a spatula or palette knife so there are no lumps or peaks.

4. Melt the remaining butter and seal the top in the usual way (step 5, page 119). Allow to cool completely, then cover before placing in the fridge, where it will keep for a week to ten days.

Potjevleesch
Serves 6–8

Essentially the potted meats so far in this section have been a single meat turned into a pâté, and you can imagine in medieval times the meat being pounded in mortars with salt and almost certainly some offal thrown in for good measure too. However, potjevleesch is a multi-meat preserve which is so ancient it was one of the earliest recipes to be written down. Indeed, the earliest recipe I can find is by William Tirel in 1302. Originating from northern France, it is a kind of terrine that in the first instance was made from chicken, rabbit and veal with some pork belly thrown in too.

The loose mixture of meats along with onions, carrots, herbs and garlic would be set with the gel from calf's foot or pig's trotters. These days, gelatine sheets are more likely to be used. It is this set jelly, along with the cooking process, that causes the meat to be preserved, and it will last for about a week, perhaps a little longer when covered and refrigerated, but is rarely left alone long enough for this to be tested! You'll find there is a lot of 'about' when it comes to this simple recipe. All the meat is boned and chopped into pieces roughly around 2cm, but some larger, others smaller.

3 large onions
6 garlic cloves, crushed and chopped
300g pork belly
2–3 large carrots
2–3 sticks of celery
3 pig's trotters, washed (see also Note at the end of the recipe)
300g chicken leg meat (breast will also do)
300g rabbit
300g veal (alternatively, replace with 450g chicken and 450g rabbit)
About 300ml white wine (or 50 per cent white wine and 50 per cent white wine vinegar – traditionally just vinegar was used)
Salt and black pepper to taste

1. Slice the onions into thin rings and pound the garlic into a paste using a pestle and mortar. Remove the skin from the pork belly (see page 30) and peel and chop the carrots into thin roundels. Roughly chop the celery.

2. Place a layer of onion rings in the bottom of a large heatproof terrine or casserole dish. On top of this lay the trotters and cover with a layer of vegetables.

3. Mix the meat together and season. Add the garlic.

4. On top of the vegetable layer place another layer of onions and then a layer of mixed meat. Then a layer of onions, more vegetables on the top of this and then another layer of meat. Continue this until you end up with a layer of meat.

5. Pour the wine until it covers the meat and cook over a high heat to bring to the boil. Scoop off any scum that forms and then reduce the heat to a slow simmer and cook for 3 hours. During this time you may need to top up with extra wine or you could use a mix of water and wine, or simply water. Allow to cool completely. You can serve the Potjevleesch directly from the terrine or dish but you can also turn it out. In northern France it is served with *frites* (French fries).

Note: The pig's trotters is a traditional touch. They are there just for the gelatine they produce, which will set the whole dish. You can replace them with 3 gelatine leaves. Simply place the sheets in a cup of room-temperature water to soak. Meanwhile, warm the wine until it is about 50–60°C (122–140°F). After 15 minutes' soaking time, dissolve the sheets in the wine before using for cooking. Alternatively, boil the trotters in water for 90 minutes, remove and use this liquid to set the jelly by mixing with the wine.

Galantine

This is a halfway house between a preserved piece of chicken and a pâté. It is essentially an ancient French dish, although it has its origins in other countries too, such as Poland. There have been a number of modern versions and you can buy it in supermarkets, ready sliced. The word 'galantine' comes from being posh! It was usually highly decorated and made a gallant table centrepiece. This version uses a boned chicken that is laid out flat, meat side up, and the stuffing is made from ground pork, herbs, nuts and olives. The whole thing is cooked in stock and then brushed in aspic.

This recipe is a lot of work, but it does make a wonderful display as well as preserving the meat for a week to 10 days, although of course it will be enjoyed long before then! A great party food, it is served sliced and goes well with salad.

1kg minced pork
4 garlic cloves, crushed
30g Supacure curing salt
1 boned chicken (about 2kg)
50g pistachios
12 stuffed olives, washed and sliced
150g lardons
2 large onions, cut into quarters
2 large carrots, thickly sliced
1 stick of celery, cut into small slices
2 pig's trotters
1–2 litres chicken stock
4 bay leaves, bruised (see page 32)
A handful of parsley

1. Combine the minced pork and garlic and 10g of the curing salt in a food processor and pulse into a paste.

2. Trim the uneven portions of the chicken to make them

square-ish and push the meat inwards from the edge of the skin all round. Sprinkle the inside of the chicken with the remainder of the curing salt.

3. Layer the pork over the inside of the chicken evenly, leaving approximately 1cm all round as an overlap. Then arrange the pistachios, olives and lardons in rows along the length of the pork; about 3–4 rows will suffice. Cover with clingfilm and place in the fridge.

4. Sterilise a muslin for wrapping. To do this, place your muslin in a saucepan and pour boiling water over the top. Simmer gently for 3 minutes before removing and squeezing out the excess water.

5. Place the vegetables, pig's trotters and herbs in a large saucepan with the stock.

6. Open out the sterile muslin and place the chicken on it. Roll tightly, overlapping the skin all around, then roll the muslin in place to form a large sausage. Twist the ends and tie off quite tightly with butcher's twine. Now loosely tie the length of the 'sausage' to keep it from gaping open. I recommend you tie it in about four places along the length. This is the 'galantine'.

7. Bring the stock mixture to the boil and then reduce to a slow simmer. Place the galantine in the stock and top up with more stock as necessary. Poach for 2 hours and check with a meat probe – the inside of the galantine should have reached 75°C (167°F) for at least 25 minutes.

8. Once cooked, remove the galantine and leave to cool completely. Continue reducing the stock until it is about a quarter of the original amount. Strain and leave to cool completely. Once the meat is cooled, cover and refrigerate.

9. As the stock cools, fat will form on the top, which can be discarded until the stock itself sets. When this happens, using a

sterile brush (simply hold your brush in boiling water for a minute or two) wash the cold galantine with the warmed-up aspic stock until completely covered. This will take some time. I have also repeatedly simply poured the contents of the dish over the meat placed on a rack with a bowl underneath. However, this will considerably cut down the shelf life. The galantine will keep, covered, in the fridge for ten days.

Chapter 9
Miscellaneous curing recipes

This chapter is a selection of projects I have completed over the years – things that do not just fit into a book on making bacon and hams but are also great fun and, importantly, preserve meat. Some of them have, at one time or another, been inspired either by trips to restaurants, things seen on television or suggested by the huge worldwide community of amateur curers and bacon makers.

On the whole, the people making their own cured products are friendly and helpful, and there is a plethora of different forums and websites you can visit to get ideas and tips, as well as downright help when you think you are in a mess. A word of warning, though: do not follow anyone's advice (including mine!) unless you are absolutely sure that what you are doing is going to be safe, edible and enjoyable! With that in mind, I have included a couple of recipes from Derek Senior, now sadly passed away, who was a complete expert when it came to curing and trying old foods anew.

Brawn
Serves 4

Also known as 'head cheese', though I can't think why except it is a bit cheesy-looking! At one time people would run to the butcher's to get brawn once the grapevine told them where to go. You have to go a long way to find it these days. Some specialist butchers and delis will stock it, though.

Brawn can at first seem a seriously gruesome dish to prepare. Tales of cutting up a head and jaw into a pan, teeth and all, tend to put people off making it, but it is really quite simple. For this recipe you need half a pig's head and three trotters. Personally, I ask the butcher to remove the half brain and eye simply because I don't like them – the brain is too fatty for my liking and the eyes, well, they seem to accuse! You can make it easier on yourself too by asking the butcher to chop the head for you, so it seems less 'heady', if you know what I mean. The art of making a good brawn is to have no pig hairs in it, and it must be as clear as possible.

The head and trotters are washed and then soaked in brine for 24 hours. I use 300g curing salt to 2 litres of water. Arrange in a plastic container and make sure everything is covered. After 24 hours, remove and rinse off any salt.

Other ingredients
2 onions, quartered
2 large carrots, sliced
1 stick of celery, chopped
1 tsp peppercorns
4 garlic cloves, peeled
1 bouquet garni of your favourite herbs

1. Add all the meat, vegetables, peppercorns, garlic and bouquet garni to a large lidded pan and cover with about 2.5cm liquid. I say liquid; some recipes call for stock, others cider, some beer and some plain water – it's up to you. This liquor will be reduced

later to form the basis of the brawn, so make sure you have a good litre or possibly a little more.

2. Bring to the boil and then simmer for 3 hours, skimming off any scum that appears and once the meat is visibly falling away, remove it all.

3. Now begins the gruesome task of removing the meat from the bones and setting aside. Some people shred the meat, others cut it up small – it's up to you.

4. Strain the stock from the cooking and simmer until it has reduced by two-thirds. Pour into a dish or container, or a fancy mould. Add the meat, packing well in; it should also be evenly distributed through the jelly.

5. Tap the dish several times, pushing down with a spoon to be sure all the meat is completely covered with the jelly. Leave to cool, then transfer to the fridge and leave to set for a couple of hours. You can tip out the brawn by dipping the outside of the container in boiling water for a few seconds, covering with a plate and upturning. Serve sliced.

Collard pork
Serves 4-6

Essentially this is a way of preserving for only a short time, using a pickle. There are many recipes for a crust to be added to the pork. Some recommend you add the crust before cooking, others not. The pork is cooked first and then brined second. This recipe is for pork without a crust.

1kg pork (a piece of shoulder is good but any cut will be fine), boned and skinned (see page 30, or ask your butcher to do this for you)
1 onion, quartered
2 carrots, sliced
1 stick of celery, chopped
1 tbsp peppercorns

Place all the ingredients in a pan and cover the pork with water. Bring to the boil and simmer for 2 hours or until the meat is tender. Remove from the water, which can be used for the next stage.

For the brining
750ml chicken or vegetable stock or water
200g curing salt
300ml malt vinegar

1. Bring the stock or water to the boil and dissolve all the salt. Add the vinegar and then allow to cool.

2. Immerse the pork in the pickle and weigh it down, so the meat is covered (I use a plate, which is usually enough). After five days, remove from the pickle, wash and pat dry with kitchen paper towels. Serve sliced. It will keep, covered, for up to a week in the fridge.

Chicken roll
Serves 6

This is Derek Senior's recipe for a chicken roll using a springform press (like a loaf tin with a lid) to create the actual roll. There is a central cylinder of sage-and-onion stuffing running through the meat, which makes it quite special. The lid is also quite special – it has a spring mechanism that pushes the meat down, pressing it. It can be used in the oven or, as in this case, placed in a pan of hot water.

Springform presses, often in the traditional oval shape, are available on the internet. Specialist kitchenware stores such as Lakeland also sell them. Here, I used one that was 10cm diameter.

3–4 tbsp sage-and-onion stuffing
1kg of chicken breast and thigh meat, cut into 1cm pieces
16g salt
½ tsp white pepper
Pinch each of nutmeg and summer savoury,
2 heaped tsp potato starch (from supermarkets or Chinese wholesalers)

Here, Derek takes up the narrative ...
'In order to get the stuffing to stay in the centre I mixed a handful of breadcrumbs, some rubbed sage and onion and sufficient water to hold it together. I then rolled it into a 3-cm log, wrapped it in clingfilm and put it in the freezer overnight.

'Following this, I then weighed the seasoning into a plastic bag. I added potato starch because I thought that with that amount of meat and a small amount of seasoning it would be difficult to mix well, so the potato bulked it out and helped to spread it around. I gave it a good shake and mixed it in with the meat.

'I then lined the mould with the supplied boiling bag, placed some chicken on the bottom and removed the film from the now-frozen stuffing. I placed it in the mould and worked the rest of the chicken round it, pressing it firmly down and fitted the spring lid.

'Due to the size of the mould the only pan large enough to stand it in was a mazlin pan [a large pan that is often over 4.5 litres in capacity and used for making cheese or jam]. I filled the pan up to the level of the mould where the meat was, which was close to the brim. Fortunately the temperature required – 85–90°C (185–194°F) – does not make the water bubble and boil over, but you have to keep topping up.

'I was looking for an internal temperature of 75°C (167°F). The instructions with the mould said to cook at that temperature for 2 hours, and I then emptied out the hot water and filled the pan with cold to stop the cooking process whilst in the cold water the internal temperature rose to 78°C (172°F).

'When cooled down it is put in the fridge overnight before removing from the mould.'

Here are the step-by-step instructions:

1. Prepare stuffing in the usual way, wrap in clingfilm and roll to make a 3cm x 18cm sausage and then freeze.

2. Mix all the other ingredients together in a bowl, mixing well to incorporate with the chicken.

3. Now line the press with heat-safe clingfilm or a boiling bag and press the chicken mixture to a depth of 2–3cm. Remove the clingfilm from the stuffing and lay the stuffing on the chicken in the press.

4. Build up the roll by adding chicken around the sides, pressing down, and finally top with a layer of 2–3cm of the chicken meat.

5. Place in a pan of water and bring to the boil. Simmer until the meat reaches 75°C (167°F) when tested with a meat probe and then cook for a further 2 hours, topping up as necessary with boiling water.

6. Cool and then refrigerate, covered, for 24 hours before turning out to serve. Serve thickly sliced with salad or thinly sliced as sandwiches.

Derek Senior's turkey and chicken ham
Serves 4–6

400g turkey (I used sliced turkey breast from the supermarket)
1kg chicken (I used thigh meat)
150g ice
18g curing salt
1 tbsp sugar
1 tsp potato flour
1 tbsp gelatine
50ml water

1. Cut the turkey meat into 1cm-thick slices and then into 5cm-long strips.

2. Remove the skin and bone from the chicken meat (see page 30, or have your butcher do this for you) and mince through a 5mm disc. Put the minced chicken into a food processor, add the ice and grind together. This makes a bit of a sticky mess but the end product is well worth it.

3. In a bowl mix the curing salt, sugar, potato flour and gelatine in the water. Mix all the ingredients together well to evenly disperse the seasonings.

4. Line a mould (Derek had a special press but you can use a 900g loaf tin) with foil and clingfilm. Add the meat mix, packing it well. Fold over the clingfilm and foil and refrigerate for 6 hours to allow the curing process to complete.

5. Preheat the oven to 180°C (Gas 4). Place the mould in a deep baking tray and fill with hot water to come halfway up the mould. Transfer to the oven for 75 minutes. When cooked, place the mould in cold water with a weight on top to compress the meat (I use another loaf tin filled with potatoes or kitchen weights). Leave to cool before placing in the fridge overnight.

6. Serve thickly sliced with salad, or thinly sliced in sandwiches.

Derek Senior's slicing pork
Serves 4–6

'In a way, this is a bit like brawn except the recipe uses gelatine instead of pig's trotters to set. I had 800g of pork shoulder trimmings left over from pie making, which I cut into large chunks. I put them in a plastic bag, along with 10g of curing salt, and rubbed it round in the bag to work it into the meat. I left this to cure in the fridge overnight.

'The next day I rinsed the salt off the meat and placed it in a pan with 2 bay leaves, 2 cloves, 1 onion (cut small) and 2 cloves of crushed garlic. I filled the pan with water about 1cm above the meat and brought it to the boil, then let it simmer for about 2 hours. I then strained the meat and removed the cloves and bay leaves and allowed the meat to cool for a while. I shredded the meat into a bowl and mixed in 1 teaspoon white pepper and half a teaspoon of ground black pepper and transferred it to a glass bowl.

'I mixed 1 tablespoon of gelatine with 300ml of the cooking liquid and added 2 teaspoons of lemon juice. This was poured into the bowl with the meat and worked in with a fork so that it permeated throughout the meat. It was left to cool and then covered and placed in the fridge overnight. The following morning I placed the bowl in hot water for about a minute to release the jelly from the bowl and tipped it out, wrapped it in clingfilm and returned it to the fridge until needed.'

This makes an easy evening meal served with boiled potatoes and a salad.

Pressed meats

These are easy to make and are completely amazing in as much as you can make them from the leftovers of the appropriate meats. Essentially you are going to separate some of the meat from a cut and set this using a gelatine stock, preferably made from bones but sheet gelatine will do. They are best pressed and allowed to set while under pressure. That way they cut more easily than if you simply plonked the meat together and then set it.

Pressed chicken

This is such an easy dish to make. I usually boil a chicken, whole (about a kilo – per kilo of chicken meat add 2 level teaspoons salt, see method). You used to be able to get boiler chickens that were very old and tough, but made great stock and had some meat on them at least. Call me a softie if you like, and I daresay if needed I would relent, but I don't like killing my own hens for meat – after all, they have given me lots of eggs, and fun!

1. The chicken is boiled with 2–3 diced carrots, a peeled onion, 2–3 garlic cloves and a little salt. Keep on a rolling boil until the meat falls off the bone (40 minutes to an hour) and sieve the stock into a separate pan.

2. Remove the meat from the carcass and leave to cool and dry. You can include the skin. The meat and skin are then pulsed in a food processor so you have small fine pieces, no bigger than a few millimetres. If you have a grinding attachment on your food processor or a hand-cranked grinder, grind using the coarse cutting plate. Add 2 level teaspoons salt and mix well.

3. If you have a press, all well and good, but if not, pack the meat as tightly as you can into the narrowest pan you have and put a saucer or a plate on the top. Some heavy weights will help form the loaf of meat. Transfer to the fridge and press in this way for a couple of hours.

4. Meanwhile, reduce the stock to about a third, add a couple of sheets of gelatine and mix well. Alternatively, boil some pig's trotters in the stock to get the same gelatinous effect. Personally I prefer the trotters.

5. Pour the gelatine into the mixture, tapping and banging the pan frequently to facilitate the transit of the liquid. Once the liquid is slightly over the top of the meat, leave overnight until set.

6. There are a number of presses you can use. Some fruit and cheese presses come with a specific general-purpose press, which is ideal for meat. You can use a couple of 900g loaf tins or

buy one of the many springform tin presses available on the internet. To recreate the same result in most cases you add your meat and jellied stock and then apply the pressure usually with a screw-clamped lid. It is important not to over-press, otherwise the amount of stock will diminish and creates a sandwich meat that will fall to pieces.

Other sandwich meats
Pork and beef sandwich meat is essentially made in the same way. Try to avoid overtly fatty cuts of meat, and do be careful when making the meat. It might be a temptation, for example, to cook a turkey for Christmas and then decide to use some of the leftover turkey meat to make pressed turkey. However, using meat that has been previously cooked and then left, possibly handled and certainly infected one way or another, is a dangerous thing. Always make sandwich meat from raw meat from scratch.

Cooked poultry and meat products need to be salted properly, thoroughly cooked and stored in a cool and very clean place such as a fridge or pantry. Always consume sandwich meats within a few days.

Bacon ribs

As a young man my favourite meal was bacon ribs, though I never knew it was 'bacon' – we just called them 'ribs'. We ate them with cabbage and home-cooked chips, salt and vinegar. They were so wonderful! I say 'were' because we don't eat them much these days – some family members cannot get over the look of a sheet of ribs. They do look rather Neanderthal, I suppose, but oh, so tasty! There are many recipes out there, and if you like eating with your fingers, they are superb for this.

It took me a long time to work out this cure because I simply could not find anything on the subject. The big problem was the fact that semi-industrial production of bacon ribs was such that they were cured in large containers in a salt cure. You bought a sheet of ribs a little like a bronto-burger that Fred Flintstone might enjoy. The butcher would break them in half with a cleaver, fold them up and wrap them. By the 1960s they were already regarded as 'cheap' food and so my mother wouldn't buy them herself, she would send me instead.

This recipe uses a simple curing salt cure of 400g per 4 litres water, though actually it wouldn't really matter if you used more because they are to be boiled, and since there is only a small thickness of meat, they should be perfect once cooked, the excess salt being removed. Actually getting a sheet of pork ribs to cure is quite difficult and you will need to find a butcher who will give you a full sheet.

400g curing salt per 4 litres of water

1. Cut the ribs to fit whatever container you are using and cover with the brine (no extra flavours are needed). Cure for two days (see also page 20) and then cook within a couple of days to consume.

2. To cook the ribs, place them in a pan of boiling water with a pinch of salt and boil for about 15 minutes, or until the meat falls off the bone easily. Alternatively, you can cook them in a pressure cooker for 10 minutes at full weight. They are best served with lots of boiled cabbage and potato chips (proper, twice-fried chips), salt and vinegar.

Note: All chippies twice-fry. To do this at home, fry the potato chips at 170°C (338°F) until softened, then drain on kitchen paper towels. Re-fry at 220°C (428°F) to crisp up.

Pies for preserving

Sumptuous, full of flavour (and hopefully with a touch of juices baked onto the pastry where it has boiled over), the best pies are salty, rich, dark and almost peeling. Then there's the fearful expectation – will the crust stand up properly? Will the jelly have formed fully around the meat? Will the seasoning be perfect? The making of pies at home is a tradition long forgotten in modern times, but the truth remains: if you want a good pie, you need to make it yourself.

One of the problems about pies is that on the whole people have become accustomed to eating the machine-made product, which by its very nature has no soul and only a little more flavour. Pies are personal, and have been created over many generations to become those we know and love today.

Of course there are many pies in the repertoire of British cuisine. With origins steeped in the open-fire cooking of the Dark Ages, pastry has undergone quite a transformation from being a protection from intense heat for meat and fish in hot embers to an integral part of the eating experience. The whole point of the pastry is that it makes an ideal way of preserving the contents of a pie. Preservation is done in three ways: cooking, encasing in jelly and finally covering in a crust. Originally the pastry crust was not only highly fatty but also rubbed in lard to cut out any air and therefore prevent any microbes from gaining access. Well, that was the theory at least. These days the coating is replaced by an egg wash, usually just for looks.

Raised pork pie
Serves 8–10

You simply haven't lived until you've become a lover of pork pie. Traditionally they are Christmas fayre, made from the trimmings of the pig as it is being butchered, and frequently this is a great way of incorporating offal into the food, too. The pies had to be prepared during Advent and were to last until Twelfth Night, which puts them well into the 'preserved' meat category.

The pastry gloss is a mix that you can buy from butcher's suppliers online. It is savoury and you just brush it on. But I never bother with this – an egg beaten together with a splash of milk is just fine.

The key to making a good pork pie is organisation and steady accuracy. Just take your time and be methodical and it will all turn out fine.

Note: Other herbs and spices to taste may be used in the filling, such as a pinch of mace or nutmeg, 1 level teaspoon of mustard powder, paprika or mixed herbs. There are lots of variations on the pork pie – basically, it's up to you. My favourite is a layered pie with chicken at the bottom, then a layer of sun-dried tomatoes and then a layer of pork on the top. Juices from the pork seep into the chicken to make it succulent and rather special. You can add oysters, anchovies, heart and black pudding … almost anything!

800g plain flour plus extra for rolling out
2 level tsp salt
400ml hot water
400g lard
Pastry gloss or egg and milk mixture to glaze

Filling
600g minced pork
600g pork shoulder (leave the skin on – it makes for a great gelatinous pie)

2 level tsp salt
White pepper to taste

Jelly
4 pig's trotters
1 onion, quartered
1 carrot, peeled and halved
2 sticks celery, thickly sliced
2 bay leaves
1–2 tsp salt
Sufficient cold water to fill the pie with about 4cm to spare at the top
Black pepper to taste

1. To make the pastry, sieve the flour and salt into a mixing bowl and make a well in the centre. Pour the hot water into a heatproof jug and add the lard. Allow it to dissolve in the water.

2. Pour the lardy water into the seasoned flour and stir well to combine with a wooden spoon. Bring the pastry together with your fingertips and gently knead to form a smooth pliable dough.

3. On a floured surface roll out two-thirds of the pastry while still warm and use it to line a greased 20cm round springform tin. Reserve the remainder of the dough to make the lid of the pie.

4. It is always a good idea to leave your pastry to rest for half an hour, but with hot water crust it is imperative. Many times I have rolled out my pastry while warm, only to have it fall to pieces while filling the baking tin. Trying to raise a warm pastry is equally impossible.

5. To make the filling, preheat the oven to 180°C (Gas 4). Meanwhile, place the minced pork in a mixing bowl. Slice the pork shoulder into 1–2cm pieces depending on taste.

6. Combine the two meats, adding the salt and pepper and any other seasonings you may wish to use (as above). Press the meat down well into the pastry shell, packing it firmly in and making sure there are no air pockets. Any air pockets will cause leakage

or even holes in the pie. You will lose juices and it will be impossible to add jelly later on, so take great care at this stage.

7. On a floured surface roll out the lid for the pie, making it a little bigger than the pie itself (measure this using the baking tin, if you like). Seal the edges, pinching them firmly together with your fingertips (a technique known as 'crimping'), or use a fork to press the pastry together. Brush the top with your chosen glaze (see above).

8. Wrap a layer of foil around the base of the pie tin and halfway up the sides to seal in the meat juices and protect the base of the pie from burning. Then place on a baking sheet.

9. Bake for 1¾ hours then test for doneness by inserting a metal skewer into the centre of the pie. If cooked, the skewer will come out clean and the juice will be clear with no traces of pink. Cook for a further 15 minutes as necessary.

10. Leave the pie to cool in the tin. When cool, add the jelly.

11. To make the jelly, wash the trotters well in cold running water. Place all the ingredients for the jelly in a large stock pan and bring to the boil. Turn down the heat and simmer for 2½ hours. For a clearer stock, every so often remove any scum that forms.

12. Remove the trotters from the stock pan, turn up the heat and reduce the stock by half, stirring, for a thick jellied stock (by a third for a thinner, softer jelly).

13. Usually I let my stock cool and set. When it is time to jelly the pie, I use a metal skewer to make a large hole in the pie crust and then slowly pour in the warm stock, letting it fill, settle and fill again. Needless to say, the smaller the pie the easier it is to get an all-round seal of the meat inside the pastry. Once sealed, the pie will last for two weeks in the fridge. Opened, it will keep for about ten days (cover and refrigerate). When you make your own raised pies you will find as a general rule they won't be around for more than 10 hours!

Individual raised pies
Smaller pies, individual size, are made in just the same way as the Raised Pork Pie recipe on page 138, but here the crust is lifted around a mould called a 'dolly'. Children used to make dolls out of the moulds, dressing them up – it was quite a thing in the eighteenth century. In my day we would wash clothes in a 'dolly' tub, a big, galvanised tub with a stick that has three legs on the end. Actually I prefer to use a jam jar, which is floured, and sometimes I put ice in the jar to keep the pastry really workable.

Individual lids are crimped onto the filled pies and after an egg wash they are cooked accordingly. You can buy butcher's pie wash, which gives the pie a real glow, with a depth of colour and a traditional flavour. Sometimes I have washed the pie in milk and sprinkled a dried stock cube on the surface – well, *I* like it! Other surface flavours may be added – peppercorns are good, mustard works well too.

Since these smaller pies have a narrower depth of meat, the cooking times need to be adjusted. Basically I test them after 40 minutes with a meat thermometer, and if they are at 75°C (167°F), I give them another 15 minutes. Keep on testing until you are happy. Leave to cool and then add the jelly and store as for the larger pies (see page 140). Individual pies are rarely left unconsumed, though!

Sausage meat
Makes 16 sausages

This is not a book about sausages, but sausage meat certainly is a good way of preserving meat. It can then be used in any number of other recipes, let alone sausages! This fairly basic recipe can be modified with flavours. From stuffing to Scotch eggs, there is plenty of scope for using sausage meat.

A good sausage meat recipe should have some important constituents. As a bare minimum it needs fat, breadcrumbs, salt and water. The fat gives flavour and a good sausage is 10 per cent fat. If you use minced pork shoulder, that quantity of fat is just about what you get. Breadcrumbs are not there to bulk out the sausage, but to absorb cooking juices. Without them you get a separation of meat and juices, which is no use at all. Butchers prefer rusk to breadcrumbs because it contains no yeast, thus increasing the keeping time of the meat. Water is there to cook the sausage, and should be around about 10 per cent of the make-up, while the salt preserves.

This recipe uses pork loin, so you can decide how much fat you are going to add for yourself. If you use pork shoulder, on average this has 10 per cent fat, which is a reasonable amount for sausages. However, some people prefer less fat, or more according to taste. Using lean pork meat allows the cook to decide exactly how much fat is added.

1kg pork loin
120g pork fat (keep very cold)
150g breadcrumbs
20g salt
6g pepper
50g each of chopped fresh sage and thyme
3g mace
100ml water

1. First, mince the pork and either mince the fat (do this while it is very cold to prevent it from smearing) or chop into very small pieces. Transfer to a mixing bowl.

2. Add the remaining ingredients apart from the water and then add the water to make a paste. You will need to judge if you need more or less water: the mixture should be stiff and sticky.

3. Transfer to a dish, cover with clingfilm and refrigerate. Do not use for 8 hours to give the flavours sufficient time to develop. It will keep for a week.

Venison roll
Serves 4

400g venison (use offcuts from any part of the animal or mince)
200g fatty bacon
½ onion, sliced and finely chopped
100g breadcrumbs
1 large egg
A large handful of chopped parsley
3g salt (any salt will do)
2g pepper

1. First, mince the meats together and then transfer to a mixing bowl. Add the remaining ingredients.

2. Flour a muslin (just spread it out and sprinkle flour on top of it) and put the meat in the middle. Draw to a ball and tie very tightly with butcher's twine. You can use a pudding bag for this, although usually I prefer to use a double thickness of muslin. (Pudding bags are available online, from large supermarkets and kitchenware suppliers such as Lakeland.) Place in boiling salted water and bring to the boil.

3. Reduce the heat and simmer for 2 hours (top up with boiling water from the kettle, as necessary), when the meat can be removed and allowed to cool before refrigeration. It will last a week, covered in the fridge, assuming no one knows it's there! This makes a great alternative to roast beef for a Sunday lunch.

Kofta
Serves 6

These salty, spicy kebabs are essentially the preserved meat of the Mediterranean, with variations, and then on through Asia to China. It is said that they were highly spiced to keep them safe to eat during long journeys along the Spice Route to the Orient and were spread around the world by Genghis Khan and his hordes. I suppose this resembles the tales about biltong (see page 88) being created from the salt of horses' sweat as the farmer rode all day long with his food tucked under his saddle, but the basic idea is that the meat was highly spiced and then placed beneath the invader's saddle and the mix of horse sweat, the weight of the rider and the spices made a meat supposedly suitable for consumption.

Kofta are similar to a kebab and may be cooked on a skewer if you wish. I strongly suggest you create a mild version, cook a little and then decide if the flavours are to your liking. My first batch was far too hot for me, but it kept a long time in the fridge!

500g minced lamb
500g minced beef
80g bulgur wheat, soaked in sufficient hand-hot water to cover and left for 10 minutes
1 small onion, sliced
1 red pepper, deseeded and sliced
2 hot chillies, deseeded and thinly sliced (or use chilli powder if preferred)
3–6 garlic cloves, finely chopped
2 tbsp pine nuts
2 tsp ground cumin
4 tbsp fresh chopped parsley
15g tsp salt
1 level tsp black pepper

1. Mix the meats together in a bowl and stir in the drained bulgur wheat when cold.

2. Place all the remaining ingredients in a food processor and blend until a paste is formed. Add a little water to loosen, if necessary.

3. Mix the paste into the meat, combining well. Massage the flavours into the meat to make a pliable mixture.

4. Form into sausage shapes about 10cm long, around metal skewers if you prefer. Cover and leave on a tray in the fridge for 1 hour before grilling, frying or cooking on the barbecue. Generally, I fry in a little oil for about 10 minutes, turning once, until browned and cooked through. If cooking on the grill or barbecue, allow 10–15 minutes, turning halfway through. Once cooked, they will last for up to a week in the fridge. Serve with lots of salad, shredded cabbage, mayo, pittas or naan bread.

Pickled heart
Serves 4–6

This is a product borne of poverty: when meat is expensive, heart is cheap. Pickled heart is used mostly to bulk out other dishes and is great with curry. Many Lancashire people loved roast heart, and in times past you would see them on butcher's trays, dressed with parsley to hide the blood.

Essentially you are cleaning the heart, dividing it into two and removing any blood before cooking it. You then slice the muscle from the sinews and other 'bits' and pickle this.

To sterilise the jars, use a sterilising fluid or boil them for 10 minutes in a large pan. Alternatively, you can pop the jars in a preheated oven (150°C/Gas 2) for 20 minutes. However, the oven is too fierce for the rubber seals of the lids, so pop these into boiling water instead.

1kg heart meat
15g curing salt
200g sugar

500ml malt vinegar
500ml water
5 garlic cloves, crushed
1 tsp peppercorns
3 bay leaves

1. First, wash the outside of the heart in cold running water then cut it into two pieces. With a sharp knife remove any blood, obvious connective tissue and any arteries you can see.

2. Place in a saucepan and cover with water. Bring to the boil and simmer until the meat is 75°C (167°F) when tested with a meat thermometer and has been so for 20 minutes. Remove from the water and allow to cool.

3. To a litre of the strained boiling liquid, add the remaining ingredients and bring to the boil to dissolve all the sugar. Allow to cool, covered, in the fridge.

4. Slice the heart into strips, cutting away any of the sinews, etc., so you only have pieces of meat. Pour the pickle into sterile jars and add the meat. Seal and refrigerate. The pickled heart will last a couple of months. Serve sliced in salads or sandwiches; you can add them to casseroles too.

Low and slow BBQ ribs
Serves 4

Yes! Barbecuing is akin to curing, although we never think of it, particularly in the UK, because the 'idea' we have about the process is to pop some meat on the hot barbecue, cook it and eat it accompanied by lots of wine and family and friends. But that is not the way in the Americas, where barbecuing is more of a religion.

The whole point is that, once cooked, and usually smoked in the process, the meat remains edible for some time, at least a couple of weeks when covered and refrigerated. Remember too that our definition of charcuterie goes beyond simple survival to making something taste quite wonderful. This recipe for 1kg of ribs works equally well with beef, pork or lamb ribs. It is a three-stage process: the rub and the cooking, and then the sauce. The sauce is an integral part of the process – it's not sauce in the way that we usually think of it.

1kg ribs
Olive oil for marinating

Rub
1 tbsp cumin seeds
1 tbsp paprika
1 tbsp curing salt
1 tbsp brown sugar
1 tbsp ground black pepper
1 tsp chilli powder
1 tbsp crushed and grated garlic cloves (5 cloves altogether)

Sauce
2 tbsp olive oil
6 garlic cloves, crushed and chopped
2 tbsp tomato purée
1 tbsp chilli powder
100ml tomato ketchup

100ml cider vinegar
50g brown sugar
2 tbsp soy sauce
1 tsp black pepper
1 tsp mustard powder

1. In a large mixing bowl, thoroughly mix together all the ingredients for the rub. Take great care to get a really fine mix. The garlic adds a little moisture and makes it a more breadcrumb-like.

2. Rub olive oil all over the meat, partly to act as a 'glue'. The 'rub' is then rubbed all over the meat to coat thoroughly. Marinate in the fridge, covered, for 24 hours.

3. In a large bowl mix together all the sauce ingredients in preparation for the cooking stage.

4. If you have a temperature-controlled barbecue, set it to 150°C (302°F). You can add woodchips to your barbecue to smoke, if liked – applewood is a good choice. Now arrange the ribs on the barbecue and cook for 40 minutes.

5. At the end of cooking time transfer the ribs to a sheet of foil and brush liberally with the sauce mix. Wrap in foil and then cook on the barbecue for a further 90 minutes. At the end of this period, remove the ribs from the foil, brush with more sauce and place on the barbecue for 15 minutes.

6. You can enjoy the ribs straight away or you can let them cool and store in a lidded container (they will last for about two weeks in the fridge). However, you may well find that you rarely have any to spare unless you make them specially for saving!

Chapter 10
How curing works

The curing process
The invention of freezing food, of refrigeration and its widespread use in the home was a Victorian one, although it became more widespread in the 1930s and it wasn't until the 1960s that it became really popular and affordable. It changed the way we look at food so profoundly that it is difficult to imagine how life used to be. How quickly milk would spoil, fish and poultry had such a short shelf life and fresh perishable foods needed to be purchased more or less every day. The more common meats such as chicken and cuts of beef were so expensive that they were only affordable once a week, or even less. Imagine then how the increasingly widespread use of curing meat, smoking and drying it and preserving with various spices and combinations of acids, from vinegar to fruit juice, had such an influence on mankind. It allowed us to get enough food, and preserve it so that it would last longer, therefore feeding us for longer.

No one really knows how it all began, and we will come back to the most common curing materials later, but to start with let's take a look at a clue in a word.

The origins of saltpetre
In ancient times it was thought by many that meat placed on certain rocks lasted longer than other meats. There was something in certain rocks that preserved meat. In fact saltpetre is simply salt from a rock (petros = rock, sal = salt). It's a short step from laying meat on stones to keeping it in salty rockpools, to extracting the materials from rocks to make what we now call cures.

I'm convinced a cookery book from 5,000 years ago would make fascinating reading. Fuelled by experience and the freedom of time that modern agriculture and curing introduced, many cuisines built up that were remarkably similar from one region to the next, though still specific to localities. Consequently you get the equivalent of ham and sausage across the globe, but no one would suggest that a South American cured meat is the same as a Chinese one.

Great civilisations bordering different regions, such as Egypt, usually took on the cooking methods of their neighbours. So, in Egypt, you had both Asian-type cuisine and African. This was also true of the preserving of meat. You can find Egyptian examples of recipes using honey as a preservative for duck meat – an Asian staple – and also of using salt, a method popular in Africa.

The first real evidence of curing came from Mesopotamia, around 3,000 BC, where they used oils, salts, smoking and cooking to create a store of meat. As might be expected of the other great civilisations of the ancient world, the Samarians and the Babylonians had their cures. The Greeks and Romans also took on the processes, in their own way, many centuries later.

How salt preserves

Salt preserves by removing water and preventing fungal spores from developing. It has a multiple effect on food. First of all, it is poisonous, directly interrupting many metabolic processes. In many cases this involves microbes having to use energy to remove sodium ions and consequently reducing the ability to reproduce. If spoiling organisms cannot reproduce, although they may still be present in the food, they are not there in sufficient quantities to render it inedible.

Second, and most importantly, salt has a strong osmotic effect. It is widely known by most students that water will move from a weak solution to dilute a stronger one. The presence of a strong salt on the surface of a microbe will drag the water from within the organism, and usually with such force as to rupture the organism's cell wall in the process, thereby killing the organism. Furthermore, this same osmosis will draw water from the meat itself to such an extent that any organism landing on the food will not be able to get enough water to kick-start its metabolic processes. Where there is no water, you cannot have life. Usually!

High quantities of salt disrupt enzyme function and also DNA replication and protein synthesis, breaking down the metabolism of the microbe. The amount of salt needed to keep microbes at bay is 10 per cent, which is much higher than the salt concentration in most foods. So salt alone is not enough to keep meat indefinitely free from microbes.

Aside from the addition of salt, food may be kept safe in a number of ways:

Shelf life
This is really important. On its own, covered and refrigerated, bacon will last for a fortnight, but no longer. Keeping food clean and separate from other foods, covered, and reducing handling is important.

Temperature
You can make food doubly safe by keeping it at less than 5°C (41°F). This slows the metabolism and with the salt makes for a great product.

Other curing chemicals
From vinegar and sugar to saltpetre, fruit acids and smoking, most curing processes are there not because they taste good, but to increase their curing capabilities. A staple of Royal Navy ships, salt beef and salt pork were packed in barrels with about 20 per cent salt. This made the meat very salty indeed, but soaking it in lots of fresh water to remove the salt was part of the preparation process.

These days we use much less salt to make hams and bacon, pastrami and salt beef. Unlike Navy pork, it won't keep for months on end but is much more convenient and palatable. The trend to reduce salt in our diet is largely on health grounds and this has led to many people gradually getting used to the flavour of bacon without that much salt in it.

How saltpetre preserves

Saltpetre preserves by oxidising microbes' cell walls and breaking down into other poisonous chemicals. When it comes to saltpetre there is a lot of conflicting information. It is quite a chemical, saltpetre. Potassium nitrate is crowded with oxygen atoms that are easily released to form explosive oxidation reactions. It is added to incense and cigarettes to keep them burning, and also used in the production of explosives.

Now there are two differing chemicals that come under the umbrella of saltpetre and in various countries only potassium nitrite is used, in others only nitrate, and still more use combinations of both. Nitrates are the general form of saltpetre, and this not only increases the osmotic pressure but the almost explosive breakdown of the molecule causes havoc with the cell walls of microbes.

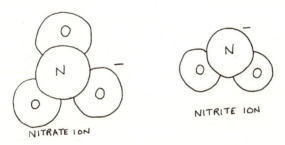

NITRATE ION

NITRITE ION

Nitrites

There is a lot of talk about nitrites. This ion (a charged molecule) interrupts the energy pathway of *Clostridium botulinum* and is therefore effective when it comes to keeping botulism at bay. The breakdown of nitrate also leads to the production of nitrite. So using nitrate can produce some nitrite, but it is not to be relied on as a way to add nitrite. The end result of the breakdown of nitrate and nitrite is nitrous oxide, which is produced in quantities to kill bacteria as the saltpetre breaks down.

Saltpetre is highly effective and is used in very small quantities in food preservation. There are a number of reasons for using it. Although saltpetre has been implicated in carcinogenic research, it is strictly controlled, although the amount you would have to consume to have problems is huge, far more than would be possible in an average lifetime. Every country in the world strictly controls the amount of saltpetre in cured products. However, it is usually compulsory to sell cured products only with saltpetre added. It is not the saltpetre itself that is implicated, but a product of its reaction with meat. Nitrosamines are chemicals formed in small quantities that have been proven to cause cancer in mice when fed vast quantities of the substance.

Types of curing salt

Some countries around the world use two different salt cures: Prague powder #1 and Prague powder #2. They are usually dyed a pink colour because one of the constituents, potassium nitrite, is poisonous.

> Prague powder #1 is 6.25 per cent potassium nitrite; the rest is made up of ordinary sodium chloride.
> Prague powder #2 is 6.25 per cent potassium nitrite, 4 per cent potassium nitrate and the rest is made up of ordinary salt.

Generally speaking, Prague powder #1 is used for curing foods that will be cooked after curing, while Prague powder #2 is used for products that will often be eaten raw. The link with Prague is the famous Prague ham produced by Antonín Chmel, which was sold worldwide and once regarded as the best ham in the world. Over time the nitrate part breaks down to give nitrite.

These pink salts are not to be used alone, but diluted with added salt according to the recipe, and it is really important you follow the recipe exactly, and also that you weigh out the materials exactly.

As the cures break down in the meat, nitric oxide is produced, which further adds to the preserving process and also reacts with protein in the meat to produce a pink colour. Hot smoke also has an element of nitric oxide and this explains the red ring effect of smoked foods.

The dilution of Prague powder with ordinary salt brings the nitrate and nitrite levels to within the legal requirements. It is therefore important to maintain the correct dilution and to be able to mix this well when producing a cure. No one wants a cure with clumps of high and low concentrations of saltpetre giving a strong cure in one place and not so strong in others.

Supacure mix curing salts
In order to save having to weigh – and, more to the point, to mix – cures, I recommend the use of Supacure, a pre-mixed salt with the exact amount of nitrite and nitrate added. Used for dry and wet cures, it takes all the calculation and the possibility of something going wrong out of the curing process. This book concentrates solely on the use of Supacure salt, which I have used for many years for successful results every time. The constituents are as follows:

> 97 per cent salt
> 2 per cent potassium nitrate E252
> 1 per cent sodium nitrite E250

Supacure is used at concentrations between 5 and 15 per cent of the weight of meat. There is no reason why it should not be used for all your meat curing needs. It is widely available on the internet and from specialist shops such as Lakeland. However, if you really cannot find it, simply look for curing salts and check that the ingredients match those above.

Different cures for different processes
Although the curing process is mostly the same, we know for example that bacon does not taste the same as ham, and that biltong does not taste like corned beef. Indeed, there are so many different cured products out there, each with its own distinctive

flavour, the home curer will accumulate a significant amount of spices and other materials.

Fundamentally all cures are the same: a mixture of salt and sugar, usually in similar proportions. Then on top of this a number of flavours are added that will give the product its particular flavour. Of course the flavour can be varied with just two ingredients because you can use ordinary salt or curing salt – there is a difference in taste. Then you could use ordinary granulated white sugar or any number of other sugars from muscovado to molasses, or even honey.

You can buy specifically designed cures to produce traditional products. Bacon and smoked bacon are popular, but you can also get cures for bresaola, corned beef, ham, tongue … almost anything. These cures are usually all-in-one – you need nothing more than the meat itself – so they are ideal for those who wish to dip their toes into the world of curing.

How much cure to use

This depends on a number of factors, weight being one of them, but also the future treatment of the product has a part to play too. Is it going to be frozen or smoked? Dried or cooked, or eaten uncooked? On the whole, it is better to err on the side of caution and not to skimp on cure, rather than take a chance.

Different recipes will have their own amounts of required cure, but in all cases the salt portion is what matters – the rest is just flavouring. As a generalisation 5 per cent of the weight of the meat needs to be added salt for a dry cure. Around 10 per cent for a wet cure, as discussed earlier in this book (see also page 76) but it needs to be emphasised once more here. Not all this will remain as salt in the product. The rub-in method of bacon manufacture, for example, will lose a lot of salt as water is drawn from the meat. Similarly, the wet cure method will not get all the salt into the meat either. What is important is that every part of the meat is cured, and when making ham, for example, this might involve having to inject cure deep into the muscle (see also page 29).

Non-salt preservation of meat

The earliest meat preservation method was drying, and mixing with fat. An Egyptian meat that was half-fat, half pounded meat was very effective – the fat being mostly impervious to most spoiling organisms. The confit as a preserving method is much the same. Meat – often duck, but not exclusively – would be cooked in herb-laden fat and when finished left to cool, allowing the fat to solidify around the meat to seal it off. Similarly, offal can be preserved in the form of pâté with fat or butter poured over the hot meat to create a seal.

Drying meat until almost all the water is driven out of it, also a common method of preserving fish, is another important way to preserve protein. It can then be eaten raw or reconstituted in cooking.

Fruits such as figs, lemons, dates, pomegranates, honey and various syrups with antiseptic herbs infused in them were once used to preserve meat for a couple of weeks or longer. Indeed, they still are in many cultures. These used acids or the osmotic capabilities of strong sugar solutions to give a measure of protection. Sometimes the acidity came from dark concoctions such as fermenting fish (still used today in the Far East and once a staple of Roman cooking too), and wine and vinegar, often in combination with other substances, were also important preservers of meat.

How sugar preserves

We use sugar in meat curing for two processes. Firstly for flavour: it permeates meat well and sweetens it, countering some of the saltiness. It also has an osmotic effect, drawing water, though not as efficiently as salt and therefore shouldn't be regarded as a replacement for salt. Honey also contains preservative provided by the bees and it is good as a confit-type covering – how it was used in Egyptian times.

How vinegar preserves

Being acidic, most vinegars work in the same way as certain fruit juices, simply reducing the microbe outer shell with free hydrogen ions. The acetate part of vinegars is poisonous for most metabolites. However, once all the acid is used up, reinfection can occur and pickled meat is frequently salted beforehand.

A word about freezing

Obviously, almost all of us freeze meat. The technique has introduced the ability to keep fresh meat fresh. However, freezing also does a number of things to meat that we do not always think about. First of all, the cold temperature – around -17°C (1.4°F) – doesn't kill the microbes in the meat, it simply holds them in suspension. They cannot reproduce and often they form cysts and shut down their metabolism. The result is a product that will appear, more or less, as fresh as the time it was placed in the freezer. If, as I have seen, people hang game for a couple of weeks, then freeze it, when the meat comes out of the cold to thaw, pretty quickly it will assume the same state it was in before it was frozen.

Freezing can be said to be virtual preserving, in as much as microbes are not killed, they are just given something else to think about. But there is a problem with freezing that we need to be aware of, and that is related to what happens to water when it freezes. Down to about 4°C (39.2°F) water increases its density, but lower than this it forms crystals which are large in comparison. This explains why ice always floats. But in a cell the ice can burst the cell walls, or even just damage them. When the meat thaws, the cell contents become liquid and the contents spill out into the tissues. These feed microbes, and they reproduce very rapidly. Keeping thawed meat for any length of time without cooking it can be a dangerous thing.

Thawed meat is no good for preserving afterward. Fully cured then frozen is fine, but do be careful.

Vacuum packing

Any fresh food can be vacuum packed. It increases the shelf life when sealed in the packet, and also cuts down on oxidation and drying, as well as the generally messed about nature of food in the fridge. Vacuum packing is also a good way of storing fish and other aromatic foods while keeping the fridge fresh-smelling. It is not preserving in itself, merely protecting the food from the action of the air. Also, it's a great way of curing smallish pieces of meat, dry-rubbed and sealed, with the cure being manipulated into the meat as the liquor is drawn from the joint. Similarly, it is a good way of flavouring meat, keeping it for longer than you would normally in a sealed environment.

I've heard that you can double the sell-by date of food with heat sealing. I rather think this gives you an extra week to be on the safe side – kept sealed and at temperatures of less than 5°C (23°F).

Chapter 11

Cuts of meat

A knowledge of what is good to buy from the butcher is really important when it comes to preserving and also in general when it comes to not buying the wrong product for the kitchen. Those more accustomed to buying from the supermarket, without a word with anyone, let alone a butcher, can hardly be expected to learn about meat.

Grain of meat

In essence, save for offal, meat is muscle, and muscle is a collection of molecular screws that take energy to twist, and, in twisting, contract the muscle. It wouldn't work if the fibres lay in any old direction, and therefore meat has layers, or a grain.

How to work out the grain of meat

Upon examination of a piece of meat, you will see the grain as layers of fibres, and although you might find it difficult to actually spot, if you place the meat on a cutting board and move it about, you will see the grain. The grain is important because the way you cut the meat has an effect on its integrity.

Cutting across the grain produces a piece of meat with at least one rough edge and smoother faces elsewhere. This is because the knife is drawn backwards over the meat, cutting or breaking through the strands. Where the strands are broken, the cut surface is 'knobbly'. It makes for two important considerations. First, the extra surface area allows cure to penetrate more efficiently. The 'knobbles' act like a sponge. Consequently, for most curing processes cutting across the grain is advisable. Also the smoking process is, in the same way, enhanced by the extra graininess of meat cut across the grain.

Pieces of meat cut along the grain are smoother in their cut surfaces and tend to have less structural integrity when cut very fine, as when making something like biltong.

The types of muscle and quality of meat

As you would expect, the quality of meat is dependent on what it has had to do when alive. Those cuts that have to work the most have more fibres per kilo, but also more connective tissue and tendons. Usually the neck works the most on all animals – they are constantly lifting their heads as they graze all day long. In a way the neck is the most nutritious meat and in some dishes the most flavoursome. Conversely, in many ways the steak cuts are often the least flavoursome, but that doesn't mean that a good steak is not tasty, or that a leg of pork can't make a great ham, because it certainly can.

Various cuts of meat

This section concerns the various cuts of meat and how they are used in curing. In recent years our methods of butchering animals in the UK are slowly turning from British to American cuts, largely because there are so many recipes that we would otherwise not recognise at all. It's fair to say that almost every country has its own peculiar butchering methods and the cooking and final preparation of food reflects the butchering. So, for example, in Argentina, whole sides of a beef carcass are tied to a framework and barbecued over an open fire for a communal evening meal. You simply wouldn't get such a cut in the UK, let alone carry it to the supermarket checkout!

This is not intended to be a guide to butchering, but aims to provide information that will enhance your knowledge of cuts so that you can make informed decisions about curing. For example, which cuts can you rely on to be lean or fatty, and what might you add to other meats or other cuts to make them behave in different ways?

Pork joints and cuts

1. Head
2. Blade
3. Spare rib and chops
4. Loin
5. Chump and leg
6. Hock
7. Trotter
8. Belly
9. Hand and shoulder
10. Hock
11. Trotter
12. Cheek

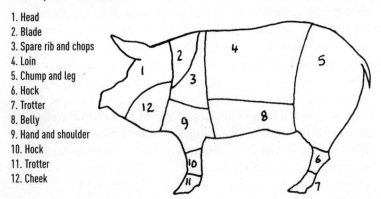

Pork is a sweet meat which requires no hanging and indeed it would be detrimental to do so. Being a 'sweet meat', pork tends to spoil more quickly. The amount of sugar it contains means that it will soon rot. After butchering it is cooled as quickly as possible so that it is ready for processing or sale. Pigs are usually cleaned out (eviscerated) and sawn in half through the pelvis, along the backbone and head. From there the animal is basically divided into three areas from which various cuts are processed.

Leg and chump

The chump is the piece of meat that goes from the pelvis two vertebrae along, and the portion is cut off at this point to leave a large leg. The chump is removed from the pelvis down as far as the pubic bone. These days the cut is not so popular; it is rather fatty compared to the leg, but not so fatty as pork shoulder.

The aitchbone is cut out with a small boning knife to give a piece of fatty meat that is often rolled for joints, but more usually minced.

Trotters

The curer's goldmine, trotters are full of bones and connective material. Consequently they give out a lot of gelatine. Roasted, they make an excellent dish but are just as important in stock making and jelly. I will boil a couple of trotters with a roughly chopped carrot and onion in enough water to generously cover the material and bring to the boil, turning down to a simmer, which continues for about 1 hour 30 minutes, making sure the water level does not fall too much.

Fat

Removing the top part of the leg from the aitchbone (which is essentially the pelvis and has the ball-and-socket joint in it) often means cutting away large quantities of fat. There are also pieces of meat that are trimmed and kept for mincing. Pork fat is invaluable in the kitchen and takes a number of forms. The fat around the hips, joints and on the shoulder meat is usually quite soft. That found on the back of the animal is much harder, often more yellow in colour due to a greater amount of sulphur in the fat, and frequently used in small pieces in sausage making. Belly fat is somewhere between the two.

There is a difference in flavour between the fats. Usually back fat is more 'piggy' in flavour than the rest, and if you render your own fat, it takes longer.

Why use fat?

In itself, fat is not cured. As you will have seen in the bacon-making sections (Chapter 3), it is not necessary to salt fatty areas so much, though this can hardly be helped when you are salting a piece of fatty meat. However, fat is frequently used as a preservative in its own right. A confit, contrary to popular television chefs, is not a dish but a way of preserving with fat – frequently duck breasts and legs in goose fat, though pork fat can also be used (see also page 164).

The meat is cooked and the hot fat it is cooked in is allowed to cool, creating a seal around the meat that forms an impenetrable barrier to microbes. The other thing about fat is that it is made from long chain molecules that are branched and very difficult for microbes to digest. Consequently, fat lasts a long time, particularly if kept cool.

How to render fat

Pork fat has to be rendered – that is, melted down, filtered and allowed to cool in a more convenient way. You see this process if you fry a piece of bacon without any oil or fat added to the pan: after a short while the fat starts to melt into the pan and is used to cook the meat.

Use the best fat you can get. In the body fat is used for a number of things: as insulation against cold, as an energy store and as a way of 'hiding' poisons because many substances are soluble in fat. The best fat for rendering comes, therefore, from organically farmed pigs, free from antibiotics and added hormones, etc.

Cut your fat into pieces of about 1cm square(ish) and place in a large pan. The key to success is to take your time. Do not allow your fat to burn – it needs to be on the lowest heat you can manage – and stir frequently. After about 15 minutes the fat will start to come away, and when you have enough to pour, you can strain it through a fine sieve into dry, sterile jars, where it will cool and set. Keep on rendering until no more fat comes out – if your fat has skin on it, you can turn up the heat at the end and make pork scratchings!

Leg

Without trotter and chump, the leg is treated in different ways depending on its destination. It can be cured bone in, and indeed is often cured with the trotter attached. However, most frequently the cut is boned with a boning knife, which is used mostly in reverse order, cutting through the seam of the muscle until the bone is reached, and then this is pared away to leave the joint, which can be rolled and tied for roasting, or cured.

Fore end

The shoulder is removed between the fourth and fifth thoracic ribs. For curing purposes, the majority of this joint is boned off for sausage making. Most butchers will make sausages on Thursday or Friday from carcasses delivered on Wednesdays, and the shoulders are either boned for sausage or rolled for joints.

The lower third portion of this joint is usually boned off except for the 'spare ribs', which are removed intact.

Hock
The hock is a cut of the lower leg, which is usually wet cured. Ham hocks are a useful starting point for many dishes, from sandwich meat to soup-laden cured gelatinous ham.

Middle
This is what is left of the carcass when the fore and leg ends are removed. Essentially it houses the belly and the loin. The loin is used most frequently for making bacon and is cut away from the ribs and backbone with a boning knife used as flat as possible. It is very lean meat, with perhaps a small amount of fat on the top edge. The muscle gives the animal its 'inner strength' and it can be up to half a metre long.

The belly is cut out from the bottom up to the breastbone and is the fattiest portion of the animal. It has many uses, from simple roasting to making bacon and sausages. Because this has the highest fat portion, the meat is perhaps the most tender of all pork cuts, but not quite – hog's face has to be the best of all!

I remove the outer skin before any processing. The cut is often sold in strips, but can be bought or butchered as a sheet.

Loin
The loin is a long strip of muscle that gives the animal its core, or inner, strength. It is good-quality meat with little fat, which is usually found on the outer edge. This is archetypal bacon meat, though the archetypal British back bacon is essentially the pork loin at one end and a small 'tail' of belly at the other.

Beef joints and cuts
There are not so many cuts of beef that are not regularly destined for the curing table, but it is still a good idea to get to

know them. On the whole, brisket and some of the steak cuts are used for curing, topside and silverside for jerky/biltong, but jerky/biltong is actually more commonly made from loin and indeed nothing would stop you from slicing skirt!

Corned beef is another brisket favourite that can be made from any other cut, so long as it is not too fatty.

1. Neck and clod
2. Chuck and blade
3. Fore rib
4. Sirloin
5. Rump
6. Topside
7. Silverside
8. Thick flank
9. Leg
10. Flank
11. Thin rib and skirt along the bottom
12. Thick rib and rib-eye
13. Brisket – goes down the chest
14. Shin

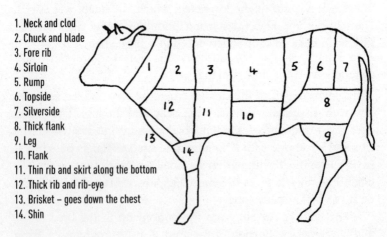

Neck
This is a cut of meat which comes from the sixth vertebra forward and involves a lot of boning out with a knife to produce a sheet. It is quite a fatty joint and is either cut into chunks for stews and casseroles or rolled into a roasting tin for long, slow cooking.

An inexpensive meat, it is full of wonderful flavours and slow cooking intensifies them.

Leg of mutton joint
Located between the neck and the brisket, it is cut and rolled to create a slow roasting joint with less sinew than the neck.

Brisket
This is the favourite cut for curing. It is a good muscle, with a reasonable amount of fat but little sinew. The muscle controls the foreleg and is removed whole. Brisket is used for bresaola,

corned beef and many other products such as jerky/biltong. It is also one of the cheapest cuts of meat you can buy.

Chuck
This cut is from the shoulder blade and usually sliced into chunks for stews or braising steak. Being slightly tougher, it needs a lot of cooking.

Skirt
Also known as the hindquarter, this cut is quite fatty and generally used for slow cooking.

Rib-eye
The rib roast, which is the first five ribs of the cow, is a joint that has a great following for roasting, but the rib-eye is the eye-shaped meat from the rib roast. Fried or barbecued, it is a firm favourite.

Rump
This is taken from the top of the rear leg, where the meat is sinewy and tough, but responds well to slow cooking. It can be used for curing, especially bresaola.

Sirloin
Located at the top of the rib cage towards the back end. Very tender, it is great for biltong/jerky.

Silverside
The meat from outside the top of the back leg. Really good for corned beef, though brisket works just as well. It can be used for all types of curing.

Topside
A Sunday roast joint, but ideal for making small amounts of cured meats. Its open-grained nature means that it can dry out on cooking, and this makes it perfect for biltong/jerky.

Poultry and game

Chickens can be the most flavoursome of meats, or the most boring. Everyone knows about the health benefits and the wonderful taste of chicken soup and this is largely due to the oils found in the meat. You can classify a chicken as follows:

Breast

Large muscles on either side of the bird. Although large, they rarely do much work and consequently are not particularly endowed with oil, making them less tasty than other cuts.

Thigh

Powerful jumping and running muscles, thighs are very moist and flavoursome. They are the man propulsions of the bird and jointed at the hip and leg.

Leg

Muscles that control the feet as well as orientating the leg. They are used as drumsticks.

Feet

Bony, with thick scaly skin, chicken feet are deep-fried in Chinese cuisine or used in stock.

Olives

Located on the underside are two small indentations near the front of the bird. Quite possibly the tastiest bits, they are the carver's treat!

Parson's nose

A gristle-filled flap near the back of the bird, this is great fried.

Carcass meat

Always there is lots of meat that can be pulled from the carcass. It is used in orientating the bird, keeping it upright. Between the myriad rib and connecting bones the meat is very gelatinous and oily.

Skin
What it says on the tin, really. The skin should never be discarded and can be roasted alone to make sheets of crisp loveliness.

Below you will find a set of instructions on how to quarter a chicken. With only minor modifications, they will work for rabbit and other game too.

Quartering a chicken

1. First, place your chicken, breast up, on a board. Use a stout pair of scissors to make a cut from the head to the bottom end and flatten out the bird. Use a boning knife to remove the breastbone.
Remove the wing tips.

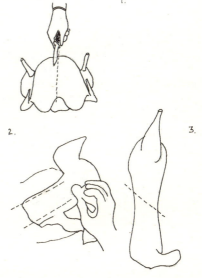

2. Using a large knife, cut through both sides of the backbone and remove it.

3. You now have two halves of a chicken. Place these skin side up and then, holding both ends, pull gently. A line will appear, which you can cut through to give you four quarters.

4. You can remove the lower legs if you prefer, and the wing inners too. All trimmings go in the stockpot.

Pigeon breast
Many home curers are keen to try their hand at shooting, and this usually means joining a pigeon-shooting club unless you

know someone with a country estate. You can pluck it, clean out the bird, and cook it whole, but in the majority of cases the breast is opened with a sharp knife and the two large muscles removed on site, the rest of the carcass being left for the crows and foxes.

Chapter 12
Notes on smoking

Smoking food at home is becoming big business. It has mostly been an American pastime, specifically since nearly all the bacon they consume is smoked, and the majority of the other hams, jerkys and even whole turkeys are treated to a whiff of smoke. Many South American countries, particularly Argentina, cook meat in such a way that it cannot avoid being smoked, over large wooden fires. The *asado*, or Argentine barbecue, is a common sight. Even motorway service stations, if you can call them motorways, have their freshly cooked and cured meats. I was particularly pleased to see the meat was always cooked at an angle, allowing the juices and fat to drip to the side and not into the fire because otherwise it imparts an acrid flavour to the meat.

There are so many different types of smoker on the market, so much equipment you could buy. It is easy to imagine ancient peoples cooking over a wood fire and enjoying the smoked flavour of their food.

Whereas smoking is not one of those processes which preserves meat in its own right, it is used in conjunction with salting and frequently after a long period of drying. You do get some preserving benefit from the smoke on the surface of the food, but the main reason for smoking, apart from the flavour, is to deter insects.

Prior to smoking, food is allowed a day or so to dry a little, forming a hardening – ever so slight, but a hardening nonetheless, called a pellicle. The smoke adheres to this, and forms a barrier which has two preserving properties. One is the chemical nature of the smoke, often resinous; it is mildly antiseptic. It also forms a crusty barrier, largely impervious to invading spoiling agents. The coating also serves to keep whatever moisture is left in the meat from evaporating and producing a dry product. Smoked cured products do have a sealed-in moistness about them.

It has to be said that these days most food is smoked for flavour. Who would buy smoked bacon if they didn't like the taste of it? The smoke is an integral part of the product. For most homemade producers the fact that smoking food gives it a few weeks' extra keeping qualities is almost secondary.

Cold smoking

Cold smoking is a way of covering food with smoke with a temperature of around 15–25°C (59–77°F), and consequently the meat is not cooked at all, just covered in smoke. In order to cool the smoke it is usually generated some distance away from the meat and either piped in or the whole process takes place in a large room, most conveniently a shed. You can make your own smoker using an old fridge and some ducting from a stove some two metres away.

There are many smoke generators available on the market which are fed by specially prepared briquettes of wood to produce cold smoke. This is frequently ducted into an old fridge, large cardboard box or specially modified shed. Just as easy, though, is setting a hook high in a chimney if you are lucky enough to have one. You need not use coal or pine, only the right kind of wood (see page 174), and don't underestimate the heat that goes up the chimney. A thermometer is an important tool in all smoking activities.

Of course you could go the whole hog and buy a complete smoking machine. At the time of writing you will pay around £300 or more for a new one, but they can be found quite cheaply second-hand. A smoking machine is a delivery system and a purpose-built cabinet combined.

All smoking is done on meat that has been cured with salt, and it is important to remember that not all smoked foods are immediately edible and many of them should be cooked prior to consumption.

Cold smoking is a four-stage process consisting of curing, drying, smoking and storing. It has to be said that homemade smokers will almost certainly never be as satisfactory as bought ones in terms of their fixtures and fittings. Perhaps this is just a reflection of my own DIY skills, but I have found the trays used in professional smokers to be ideal for the job whereas the racks I have put together myself are not so good. Homemade solutions to smoking are often quite ingenious, however. I have seen a firebox on an old wood-burning stove, a 10-metre length of ducting to a galvanised burning bin (the kind used in the garden for burning old rubbish) into which the smoke was delivered via the flue in the bin lid.

One of the things you will need to avoid is sudden changes in temperature. Too hot a smoke warms the meat, decreasing its overall keeping quality. Ten hours at 30°C (86°F) smoking time will play havoc with any poorly cured pockets of meat, the bacterial count rocketing. A good meat thermometer is a wise buy and a great tool when it comes to feeling secure about the safety of your food. Smoke at 15°C (59°F) is what you are looking for.

DIY smokehouses

Of course, many people take a DIY approach to smoking. As mentioned, you can convert old fridges, sheds, even dustbins into smokers if you are able to separate the smoke source from the food. I have seen, though never used, a system where an old shed was supplied with smoke through a steel drainpipe from across the garden, where a fire pit provided the smoke. By the time the smoke had travelled up the buried drainpipe and into the smoking chamber, some 3 metres away, it was quite cool.

The same arrangement can easily be set up with a smoke generator, as supplied by Bradley and many other companies (details online). Take time choosing what you need – there are so many different machines and ways of using them out there. Surf the internet, watch various online videos and be sure to obtain information relevant to your country – American-style smokers are quite different to British ones, and so on around the world. There isn't a great deal of room here to discuss smokehouse design, but there are a number of important factors to be taken into consideration.

First, make sure the smokehouse is easy to clean – easier said than done! What tends to happen is that the smokehouse is used (especially in the UK) in the winter and early spring months, maybe a bit of autumn too – say from October to March – then it is hardly used for months. Pieces of meat, fish, sausage and goodness knows what else can fall during the process and the laws of chaos determine that these pieces are completely invisible. All kinds of 'critters' can gain access and this can be quite off-putting.

Second, your smokehouse should have easy access with removable 'beams' of dowel or something to hang the meat. It should be constructed to cope with the heaviest piece of meat you are likely to prepare.

Third, if it is a combination of cold smoker and hot smokehouse with a fire pit in the bottom, you need to have firebricks lining the inside and a concrete roof. I once made a smoker with a slate roof, which exploded as the water caught in the layers boiled and blew the slate to pieces. It went off like a rocket!

Fourth, a wooden structure should have a pitched roof with a vent in the top with its own cover too. Another vent in the eves, with a fitted door – which can be a piece of wood or leather, nothing special as long as you can open it – is important. These vents can be left closed to build up the smoke, then opened to allow a fresh movement of smoky air.

Don't be tempted to use the smokehouse as a storage facility. Once used, clean it out, close it up and go and have a shower.

Woods for smoking

You can buy briquettes online that are specially designed for various smokers. Ash, hickory, oak, birch, pine, tea and sandalwood will all give specific flavours to the food. You can, of course, use wood shavings, but do be aware that you will need quite a few shovels full of these if you are going to smoke for six hours.

In a homemade smoker a small fire is started, preferably with charcoal, and is then smothered with shavings or dust. Alternatively, wood of the desired type is burned, and then kept with as little oxygen as possible so that it smokes. This smouldering and smoking sometimes must be maintained for up to eight hours and the temperature of the smoke tested to ensure it is still cool. You will need to experiment with quantities and times to find a method that works for you. Do a dry run, and that goes for your homemade equipment as well as your brand-new bought kit.

Wood types and their flavours vary considerably, as does the way the wood is prepared. A new, green wood will produce a different smoke to a dry, seasoned one. New wood has a lot of moisture and contains various chemicals that can add an acrid flavour. This is particularly true of rose. Here is a quick guide to the various woods:

Alder – This is used almost exclusively with fish, particularly salmon, but I have also used it to smoke burgers with great success.

Apple – A sweet wood, and at its sweetest when freshly cut. It is also relatively mild. Apple also does not give an acrid flavour when new.

Cherry – This is a fruity, resinous wood when fresh, with a sweet flavour.

Hickory – An excellent flavour for stronger meats and sausages. It is quite pungent.

Maple – People usually describe this as a sweet wood for smoking, similar to maple syrup.

Oak – This is a brilliant, strong flavour for bacon.

> *Rose* – A very fragrant and strong flavour, rose is good to mix with other woods for added body.
>
> *Tea* – Often a well-liked source of smoke. Personally I find it a little strong and you cannot always be sure of all the flavours. Earl Grey, which contains bergamot oil, does give an interesting flavour, though.

It is very rare, generally, to use resinous woods for smoking (the fragrance resembles pine disinfectant!). Conifers give a mild pine flavour, although some ham from the Black Forest is smoked in juniper for several weeks. It is also not uncommon to mix woods to create a smoke that exactly fits the product, oak and apple being a common mix for ham.

You can buy wood shavings and briquettes from most large garden centres and also online, where the variety of woodchips is enormous – you can even get whisky-flavoured woodchips (a complete waste in my view!).

How to cold smoke

Once you are able to deliver smoke at the correct temperature you can try your hand at smoking for real. Remember in the summer it is frequently too hot to cold smoke, the temperature of the air being well in excess of 25°C (77°F), and the inside of the smoking chamber is often higher still. The best time of the year is autumn or winter, during a dry period.

Make sure your meat is properly cured with salt, whatever way you prefer, or according to the recipe. When it is finished, wash the surface of the meat, finishing off with a vinegar wipe using a piece of kitchen paper. Then pat the whole surface dry.

The meat is then left in the fridge for a few days (I usually manage about three days). The salt and flavours inside the meat continue their transit through the tissues, continuing the curing process. The outside of the meat will harden a little, creating the surface more likely to accept smoke, known as a pellicle (see also page 171). The meat should be regularly turned so the portion touching whatever it is being stored on can be open to the air. It is best if you can hang the meat in the fridge, though I tend to use a bowl.

The meat is then transferred to the smoke chamber and the process begun. I use a butcher's hook to hold the meat in place. Start slowly, checking the temperature. Smoke delivery systems have temperature control, but it is always best to keep a check on it and be sure your temperatures are within parameters.

Keep checking the temperature of your meat throughout the process, and if you are using a smoke delivery system, be sure you have the appropriate number of briquettes stacked for use. Always refer to the manufacturer's instructions.

Cold smoking for everyone

A new product on the market as we go to press makes smoke with no increase in temperature for up to ten hours. The Pro Q Cold Smoke Generator is a stainless-steel tray with what looks like a maze of corridors inside. Actually the corridors make a spiral to the centre of the tray. A candle lights the powdered wood at the outermost part of the tray and, once lit, it is removed. The dust burns with a really low temperature, and so long as there is a draught to keep it lit, it will burn slowly round the track, smoking your food.

Obviously, you need a metal container with a lid that is deep enough to put the smoker in the bottom, the food at the top and enough space between to maintain cool temperatures. A lidded barbecue is ideal.

Light smoking

This is perhaps the cheapest way to smoke anything. Using a bee keeper's hand smoker, you can create a cool smoke, which you trap in a container containing your food. I started this process to smoke fish, but it works very well with thin meats such as jerky. Once cured, the strips are laid out in the largest bowl we possess and a lid goes on the top to seal it. I happen to be a beekeeper and have a smoker to quieten the bees, but as a smoking tool they are well worth the money.

Simply start the fire going inside the smoker with paper and pieces of appropriate wood (such as apple, which contains less tannin so it doesn't taste like an extremely strong cup of tea). This can prove an art in itself, but once mastered it becomes second nature. I have found a gas cooker lighter to be the easiest way (the type that gives you a small flame at the bottom of a long tube). Don't consider using firelighters – they smell like petrol and can taint the meat, even in the tiniest quantities. Once lit, give a few puffs to get a stream of cool smoke and then fill the bowl with smoke. Place the lid on, and then wait ten minutes before repeating. Actually, you can leave it even longer, just remember you are burning wood all the time in your smoker. This method gives you a light smoking, but a very definite one.

You can move the meat around between blasts, and since the jerky is already cured and dried, taste it to see if it is smoked enough. This simple method gives you an ongoing smoking that, although time-consuming, is also easy and extremely visible, as well as being inexpensive. You can use smoking wood chips or pellets as well as any wood you have available – I have a large amount of dried applewood that I use for smoking in this way.

Powdered smoke

It is possible to buy powdered smoke, which adds nothing to the preserving process but does give a smoky flavour. As with everything, start with small quantities in your cure and build up. You will then get a good idea as to what is best for you.

Just add it to your cure and apply, though in truth it is much more successful with sausages than larger pieces of meat. This is because the amount of powder you need to make it work varies. In a sausage you can add a measured amount and the whole sausage will taste of it, but a large piece of meat needs to be covered over a large area and the powder doesn't penetrate the meat, it sits on the top. Cold smoking a large piece of meat is a slower process and a lot more bother, but you get a far more even spread, better penetration and the smoke will deter insects too.

There is a lot of powdered smoke in all kinds of flavours available for purchase online but they are by no means organic. If you really must have a smoke flavour but have no way of producing the smoke yourself, you can use them. Usually based on maltodextrin (modified starch, usually powdered and mildly sweet), in minute quantities, they do the job well. To be honest, I'd rather not bother. First, it is not authentic so I could simply buy the product off the shelf. Also, it sometimes has an artificial flavour and a surprisingly large amount of it is necessary to achieve a good result. I believe the time spent getting to know how much to add is better spent learning how to smoke in the first place!

Hot smoking

In this system the smoking chamber gets hot and cooks the food while imparting a smoked flavour. This allows me to make bacon and smoke it easily in slices. The slices can then be eaten directly in the British way, with egg, or cooled and cut into pieces and added to other dishes. I have cooked lardons in this way, taking them directly to the carbonara sauce.

There are many ways of hot smoking. Use a barbecue, lighting the charcoal and then sprinkling the appropriate wood on the top, or buy a hot smoker, which is a lidded steel box with a grill tray inside. Wood shavings are sprinkled in the bottom, the meat arranged on the grill and the lid in place. The box is placed on the heat source and the shavings burn to give smoke. It is usually best if the food is put on a tray or some foil to catch the drips of oil and fat that might actually set the shavings alight or to catch the juices that could put out the lightly smouldering wood.

Fat or oil burns to give a bitter flavour you should avoid. If I am using the barbecue to smoke, I stand the meat on a rack above a tray to catch any juices and it is inspected and removed regularly.

Using a hot smoker is a very efficient way of cooking. It is remarkable how little smoke is emitted from the box. Just be careful handling it – it gets really hot. Cooking times are in the order of ten minutes for sliced bacon, fifteen for chicken breasts.

A gas-powered temperature-controlled smoker is the top of the range for serious hot smokers. On the whole they cook like an oven but with a plate on which wood is added to give the smoke. You might be asked, for example, to smoke pastrami at 160°C (320°F) for 1 hour 30 minutes and you set the smoker off accordingly. On the whole those who use these machines tend to cook turkeys in barbecue sauce with a hickory smoke and other such dishes for consumption at parties.

We use our hot smoker for bacon and smoked ordinary sausages, which are fantastic, especially with a few chilli flakes in the wood – but watch your eyes, and don't breathe in the fumes! For this we use a metal box hot smoker, placed on barbecue charcoal as a heat source, and should we wish to hot smoke anything larger, we use the lidded barbecue. These are quite successful and I have never felt the need to spend lots of money on my smoking projects.

Dutch oven

This is a brilliant piece of kit, with a large, heavy pan and lid with a large handle. There are three short legs on the bottom and the pan is placed on a campfire or the charcoals of a barbecue. You can cook all kinds of food in it from casseroles to bread and pies, and of course you can use it for smoking too.

All you need is a centimetre of wood chips in the base of the pot and then a grill on which you place your meat. It is important that the meat is either low in moisture, such as jerky, or is not allowed to drip juices onto the chips. This is achieved by putting a foul boat between the grill and the chips to collect the drips. The foul boat can be an aluminium tray or a heat-resistant dish. It sits on the wood and the drips fall onto it rather than on the chips. The drips are unlikely to catch fire but they give a bitter flavour when they burn off as smoke.

Place the lid on the pan and set on the heat source and forget about it. The wood chips on the bottom will smoke for an hour or so, plenty of time to cook most thinly cut meats with a good smoke – ideal for jerky, bacon made from pork belly and unrolled shoulder to be finally rolled to a bacon joint.

A Dutch oven is a truly amazing piece of kit. It's so old in design yet so very versatile too: use it to cook roasts, bread, cakes and smoke. You can create the most fantastic pork and beans in it too. Why we need regular ovens, I don't know, but that's the caveman in me speaking!

In conclusion

Smoking, like curing, cheese making, growing vegetables, preserving fruit and baking bread, represents a world of discovery. It can take a lifetime to master but the novice is rewarded straight away. Always keep a note of what you did, especially whether or not it worked, and how you might change things next time. Try using different types of wood, altering the temperature and the length of smoking time.

This book has been written as a pointer and not a hard-and-fast set of rules. Of course we must cure and smoke safely and we need to do it well, producing delicious treats, but more than anything, we need to do it our way, not my way or anyone else's way. So as you master the art of smoking, bear this in mind: you are in control and learning at the same time.

Index

A
additives, food 3
air-dried beef 99–102
air-dried ham 18
    Bayonne ham 70–1
    Parma ham alternative 66–7
    prosciutto 61–6
American corned beef 90–2
American hot smoked bacon 38
aprons 12

B
bacon
    dry curing 33–9
    how it is made 16–17, 25–6
    shelf life 152
    testing cured 29
    wet curing 23, 29–32
bacon and butter bean casserole 45
bacon, brie and beef tomato toasts 40
bacon ribs 135–6
bacon-topped mushrooms 41
bacon-wrapped fish 48
barbecued ribs 148–9
barbecues 1–2, 95, 148–9, 177, 179, 180
    see also hot smoking
Bayonne ham 70–1
bee keeper's hand smokers 177–8
beef
    how to make biltong and jerky 96–9

    how to make bresaola 99–102
    how to make corned beef 88–92
    how to make corned beef pastrami 94–5
    how to make ox tongue 102–4
    how to make pastrami 93–5
    how to make pressed beef 95–6
    joints and cuts 165–7
biltong and jerky 88, 96–9
boning knives 5–6
brawn 127–8
bresaola shooter sandwich 108–9
bresaola 99–102, 166
brine pumps 12
broccoli and bacon bake 46
buckets, food-grade 23
butcher's knives 6

C

Canadian bacon 31
carbonara, pancetta 57
casserole, bacon and butter bean 45
chain gloves 7
charcuterie 1, 3
cheddar, gammon and leek bake 44
cheesy bacon bake 49
chef's knives 6
chicken breast, pancetta-wrapped stuffed 56
chicken cuts 168–9
chicken galantine 123
chicken liver pâté 112
chicken, pork and sun-dried tomato terrine 47–8
chicken, potted 120
chicken, pressed 134–5

chicken, quartering a 169–70
chicken roll 130–1
cider ham 81–2
classic pastrami on rye 107
cleavers 6–7
clothing 4, 12
cold smoking 16, 172–3, 176–7
    biltong 97–8
    Croatian Pršut 70
collard pork 129–30
confit 111, 114–16
confit duck 115–16
corned beef 88–92
corned beef layer 105
corned beef stuffed tomatoes 106
Croatian Pršut 70
curing 1–2, 155–6
    chemicals 13–15, 152
    dry 20, 21
    following American recipes 21–2
    honey and syrup 24
    how much cure to use 157–8
    how Prague powders work 154–5
    how salt preserves 151–2
    how saltpetre preserves 153–4
    how sugar preserves 157
    how vinegar preserves 157–8
    injecting cures 24
    origins of 150–1, 157
    salt 13–14, 21–2, 151–2
    Supacure 21–2, 155
    wet 20, 21, 22–3
cuts of meat

beef 165–7
  meat grain 160
  muscle and quality 161
  pork 162–5
  poultry and game 168–9
cutting boards 7

D

dehumidifiers 99
dry curing 20, 21, 33–6
drying meats 9–10, 99–102
  see also air-dried ham
duck 114–16
duck rillettes 116
Dutch ovens 180–1

E

Elenski but 68–9
enzymes 3
equipment 2, 4–12, 15
everyday dry cure bacon 34
everyday wet cured bacon 30

F

fat as preservative 110, 114, 163
fish, bacon-wrapped 48
food mixers/processors 8–9
freezing meat 158
fruits as preservatives 157

G

galantine 123–5
gammon 19, 20

   see also bacon; ham
garlic pickle bacon 32
gelatine 83, 162–3
gloves 4, 7, 12
grain of meat 160
grinders 8–9
Guanciale 71–2

H
ham
   basic boiled ham cure 77–8
   Bayonne ham 70–1
   best pig meat for ham 76–7
   cider ham 81–2
   Croatian Pršut 70
   dunking a ham 79–80
   Elenski but 68–9
   equilibrium in forming cured ham 78
   glazes 80
   how it is made 19–20
   how much cure to use 78–9
   how to cook 80–1
   jambon d'Ardennes 67–8
   Parma 66–7
   Prague 69–70
   roast 71
   shank 82–3
   smoking 78
   use of brine pump 79–80
    see also bacon; pancetta; prosciutto
ham hock terrine 84–5
ham, leek and cheese layer 85
hand grinders 8–9

hats and hairnets 12
heart, pickled 146–7
herbs and spices 14
honey and syrup 24
honey bacon (whole in a bag) 37
hooks, butcher's 11–12
hot smoking 155, 179–80
    hams/bacon 22, 38–9, 69–70
    pastrami 93, 95
hygiene 4, 12, 174

I
injecting cures 24

J
jalapeño bacon 35–6
jambon d'Ardennes 67–8
jerky 96–7

K
knives 4–8, 15
kofta kebabs 145–6
kosher salt 21

L
lentil and bacon soup 42
light smoking 177–8

M
maple wet cured bacon 31
meat, choosing 76
meat slicers 11
moulds and presses 9

mushrooms, bacon-topped 41
muslin (cheesecloth) 11

N
neoprene gloves 4, 12
nets 12, 69
nitrites and nitric oxide 153–5

O
offal 110, 111, 146–7
ox tongue 102–4

P
pancetta 50–1
   how it is made 17–18, 51–5
   pancetta arrotolata 54–5
   pancetta tesa 53–4
pancetta carbonara 57
pancetta pasta with peas 60
pancetta with mixed vegetables 59
pancetta with mushrooms and Parmesan 58
pancetta-wrapped stuffed chicken breast 56
Parma ham alternative 66–7
pasta sauce, tomato and bacon 43
pastrami 93–5
pastrami and tomato sauce 108
pastrami on rye 107
pâté 8, 110–13
pea and ham hock soup 86–7
pestle and mortar 11
pickled heart 146–7
pickling meat 129–30, 146–7
pickling spice 91

pies for preserving 137–41
pigeon breast 169–70
pig's trotters 162–3
pink salt 13, 21–2, 154
pizza, prosciutto and roasted tomato 74–5
pork fat 163–4
pork joint and cuts 162–3, 164–5
pork pâté 113
pork pies 138–41
pork rillettes 117
pork, slicing 133
potassium nitrite 13
Potjevleesch 121–2
potted beef 118–19
potted chicken 120
poultry and game 167–70
powdered smoke 178–9
Prague ham 69–70
Prague powder 1 and 2 13, 21–2, 154
preserving in fat 110, 114
pressed meats 9, 95–6, 133–5
prosciutto 69
    boning and salting 63–5
    drying 65–6
    how it is made 18–19, 61–6
    using salt 62
    which joint to use 63
prosciutto and roasted tomato pizza 74–5
prosciutto-wrapped prawns and vegetables 73
pulse function 8

Q
quick pastrami and tomato sauce 108

R

rendering pork fat 164
ribs, bacon 135–6
ribs, BBQ 148–9
rillettes 114, 116

S

salt 13–14, 20, 21–3, 26, 62, 151–2
salt liquids 15
saltpetre 150–1, 153–4
sandwich meat, ham shank 83
sausages/sausage meat 8–9, 142–3
scales 10–11
shank of ham 82–3
sharpening knives 5
slicers, meat 11
slicing knives 6, 7–8
smoking/smoked meats 171–2, 181
   biltong 97–8
   cold smoking 16, 70, 97–8, 172–3, 176–7
   Croatian Pršut 70
   DIY smokehouses 173–4
   Dutch ovens 180–1
   hams/bacon 16, 17, 20, 22, 28–9, 38–9, 69–70
   hot smoking 22, 38–9, 69–70, 155, 179–80
   jambon d'Ardennes 68
   light smoking 177–8
   pastrami 93, 95
   powdered smoke 178–9
   Prague ham 69–70
   smoke generators 172
   woods for smoking 174–5
soup, lentil and bacon 42

soup, pea and ham hock 86–7
soy sauce 15
spices and herbs 14
steels, using 5
sterilisation 4, 7, 15
stock 162–3
sugar 14, 24, 28, 157
Supacure curing salt 21–2, 155
syrup and honey 24

T
temperature, storage 152
thermometers 12, 173
tomato and bacon pasta sauce 43
tongue, ox 102–4
trotters, pig's 162–3
turkey and chicken ham 132

V
vacuum packing 158–9
vacuum sealing 10
venison roll 144
vinegar 15, 157–8

W
wet curing 21, 22–4
    American corned beef 92
    bacon 23, 29–32
    ham and gammon 20, 22–3, 69–70
    Prague ham 69–70
Wiltshire cure 23
woods for smoking 175–6
Worcestershire sauce 15

How To Make Your Own Sausages
Paul Peacock

Available to buy in ebook and paperback

Beginning with the history, the significance and the flavours of the great British Banger, this book goes on to explain how to make sausages at home, with step-by-step instructions and mouthwatering recipes from all over the UK. It is ideal for those beginners who just want to make a couple of pounds for the family freezer, but it also assumes that readers will want to progress and so the necessary equipment and materials are explained, from how to buy them, to how to maintain them.

Making your own delicious sausages – from traditional Lincolnshires and Cumberlands to continental favourites such as salami and chorizo – will take you back to a time when they were always made by hand, always filled with the best ingredients, and tasted so much better than any other food stuff anywhere.